THE FREEDOM PROJECT

HOW TO FIND CONTENTMENT IN A CRAZY WORLD

Eleanor O'Rourke

Like a bird on a wire.
Like a drunk in a midnight choir.
I have tried,
In my way,
To be free.

—LEONARD COHEN

For
My Mother
and for all our mothers

CONTENTS

PART 1   A SORT OF JOURNEY   **1**

Introduction   3

SECTION 1   LOOKING FOR FREEDOM IN A COOL CAREER   **7**

Chapter 1   It was the summer of '69   9

Chapter 2   Just kids   15

Chapter 3   And they say that a hero will save us   23

Chapter 4   Machine Head   29

Chapter 5   I am an anarchist   35

SECTION 2   LOOKING FOR FREEDOM IN LOVE   **45**

Chapter 6   The future is feminine   47

Chapter 7   I am a woman in love   53

Chapter 8   What fresh hell is this?   61

Chapter 9   The tyranny of comparison   67

Chapter 10   Total eclipse of the heart   73

SECTION 3   LOOKING FOR FREEDOM IN SPIRITUALITY   **83**

Chapter 11   In case of emergency, break glass   85

Chapter 12   Must be the season of the witch   93

Chapter 13   Witchy woman, see how high she flies   99

Chapter 14   Workshop Woe   105

Chapter 15   The gut ... it's all about sex and money   111

SECTION 4   CALL OFF THE SEARCH   **121**

Chapter 16   Identity 3.0 – Real You   123

Chapter 17   Choice 3.0 – Real Love   129

Chapter 18   Story 3.0 – Real power   133

Chapter 19   Camelot revisited   137

Chapter 20   Energy – the future   143

PART 2   HOW TO LIVE IN A WORLD MADE OF ENERGY   151

Chapter 21   Walking the wire to freedom   153

Chapter 22   Spell breakers for the mind – freedom from
              stress – The Child   165

Chapter 23   Spell breakers for the heart – freedom from
              anxiety – The Lover   171

Chapter 24   Spell breakers for the gut – freedom from
              depression – The Sorcerer   179

Chapter 25   The Mantras   187

Chapter 26   The virtual Monolith   191

Chapter 27   Hey, hey we're the Monkeys   199

Chapter 28   Rage. Adoration and the invention of Cool   203

Chapter 29   How life works   209

Chapter 30   David Bowie – the day the music died   213

PART ONE

—

A Sort of Journey

INTRODUCTION

We are storytelling creatures and the life we live is a story in itself.

For thousands of years, the story we have resonated with the most is The Hero's Journey. In this story, the protagonist leaves the safety of home and travels into the unknown, in search of freedom, adventure and glory. He faces dragons, storms and people who want to kill him. He defeats them all, finds the gold and returns home to live a life of contentment.

The modern version of this story (which now includes women) looks like this...

1 We set a goal e.g. a high status job, amazing partner, or lots of money.
2 We overcome obstacles by doing whatever works (compliance, cunning, dogged determination).
3 We destroy the competition. (Also called smashing it/nailing it or just #winning)
4 We feel empty (Winning brings only fleeting joy/people are only impressed for 15 minutes.)
5 We immediately have to set a new goal.

We're now beginning to realise that, as a blueprint for life, this story has flaws. If the goal is at the end, the prize is permanently in the future. But the future doesn't exist because as soon as you get there it's the present, and there's a new future. This Hero's Journey can lead us into a life where we're always trying to reach the end, trying to get somewhere else, and trying to get there as quickly as possible. This means we're never really "here"… where life is actually happening.

A winning attribute of the hero is decisiveness. Trailblazers separate everything into good/bad, right/wrong so they can make quick decisions. We've been raised to admire decisive people, whether that's a colleague choosing a website font or the President of America choosing to bomb Iraq.

If, on the other hand, we understood the value of stillness, we could access a higher intelligence beyond these either/or options. Instead of "Times Roman or Comic Sans?", the answer might be "Maybe we don't need a website". Instead of "Bomb or Don't bomb?", the answer could be "Let's build some schools and playgrounds, then the kids might take *Terrorist* off the list of things they want to be when they grow up".

The Hero's Journey is more difficult these days, because a small number of people (collectively called The Man*) have grabbed all the prize money and gone rogue.

The Man
Words change their meaning over time. Prior to the 1960s the owner of a factory/farm/business was called The Boss. The Boss earned more money, and had the power to sack his employees. After this, capitalism went bonkers leading to global corporations owned by a small number of people who had absurd wealth, and the power to destroy the world. Meanwhile Bruce Springsteen became "The Boss" and is universally loved as a great guy.

"The Man" is happy to profit from human misery. He thinks of himself as entitled, special and superior to others, therefore sees no reason to help alleviate their suffering. Examples of The Man are found in the aristocracy, corporations, governments, and old world religions.

Currently we're surrounded by evidence of a chaotic world whose systems are collapsing. Just as the agricultural age gave way to the industrial age and the industrial age gave way to the technological age, we are on the verge of a new era, which we could call the energy age.

Science has revealed that although we appear to be physical, we're more energy than matter. Our male or female identity is like the small tip of an iceberg. Beneath the surface, our vast energy has both masculine and feminine components. For years we've favoured our masculine energy – goal oriented, productive and controlling and we've suppressed our feminine energy – intuitive, collaborative and feeling.

We see the imbalance this has caused in the world (profit over people and the environment), and we feel the imbalance this has caused in ourselves (stress, anxiety and depression).

Balancing our masculine and feminine energy would allow us to become the heroes of a new story, in which we join forces and consign The Man to the history books. In this story, we go beyond our narrow identities, so we can give full expression to "who we really are," and we rise above the limited duality of either/or, to access the higher realms of creativity, love and freedom.

In the technology age, freedom was all about escape, but freedom in the energy age is different. It's the ability to own our power of choice, without being paralysed by the fear of consequence. Imagine a life without the regret of wishing we'd done something different and without the exhaustion of constantly trying to become someone different...

That's real freedom.

I didn't realise this for a long time. I looked for freedom in all the wrong places. This book reveals some of them. It spans 50 years from the Summer of Love in 1969 to the current craziness of 2019... half a century that changed the world beyond all recognition. It's a love letter to Millennials who don't have a lot of time to make the world a better place, and a love letter to Baby Boomers who inadvertently messed things up while trying to figure these things out...

We didn't know about the energy. We thought life was all about how things looked on the surface, so we ended up re-arranging a lot of deckchairs on the Titanic.

Sorry.

Looking for Freedom in a Cool Career

ONE

It was the summer of '69

In the summer of 1969, David Bowie released *Space Oddity*.

In the summer of 1969, American astronauts landed on the moon. It wasn't the moon landing that influenced Bowie to write the song, it was the Stanley Kubrick film *2001 A Space Odyssey*.

The film opens on a wilderness, 100,000 years ago. Tribes of apes are shrieking and fighting each other. Night falls, and while they are asleep, a strange black monolith appears. The apes gather around and touch it, causing a huge leap forward in evolution. Presumably this is the "missing link" scientists are still looking for – the moment when early man developed a neo-cortex and became conscious.

This moment in our ancient history has been interpreted a few different ways...

The religious perspective

Adam and Eve lived in the Garden of Eden, they were naked (just like animals) and had all their needs taken care of... as long as they didn't eat from the Tree of Knowledge. Once they did so, they became conscious. This meant they could create (just like God). For this arrogance and disobedience, God expelled them from the garden and they had to fend for themselves. They were suddenly embarrassed by their nakedness (with consciousness comes self consciousness). They went on to create many things, some good, some bad, depending on your point of view.

The scientific perspective

In 1859 Charles Darwin published *On the Origin of Species*, in which he concluded that humans evolved from apes to Neanderthals and Neanderthals to Homo Sapiens. Unfortunately now that we have more evidence, it seems the length of time evolution would need to achieve this feat, doesn't fit with the timeframe available. Something must have happened to speed matters along – an event or a miracle, depending on your point of view.

The metaphysical perspective

What Darwin didn't know, at the time of his writing, was the fact that there are 30 billion planets in our galaxy, and there are 100 billion galaxies in the observable universe. Thinking that we are the only intelligent life in the universe is pretty absurd. Knowing how far we have come in the past 50 years means that even if a species were only 50 years more advanced than we are, they could have technology beyond what we can currently imagine... and that's just 50 years, what about 500 years? Would it be so far fetched to imagine that more intelligent beings intervened in some way to cause the leap forwards?

Regardless of our perspective, most people agree that humanity needs to take another leap in evolution, because our current way of living is unsustainable. We need more wisdom for our complex problems, more compassion for the inequality, and more respect for the environment that we all share.

So back to 1969, the last time everyone got excited about energy and the possibility of a great leap forward in evolution. No black monolith appeared, but via a strange phenomenon 100,000 hippies converged in the small district of Haight-Ashbury in San Francisco all talking about peace, love and dropping out of the old system.

There was a revolution in human consciousness as people realized the absurdity of their previous beliefs... that ethnic minorities, homosexuals and women were all inferior to white men! As the civil rights movement gathered momentum, feminism and gay liberation kicked off.

There was an explosion of creativity in music – Grateful Dead, Janis Joplin, Jimi Hendrix, Jefferson Airplane. Even established musicians changed their tunes. The Beatles went to India to meditate, ditched the suits for kaftans and brought out *Sgt Pepper*, *All you need is love* and *I am the Walrus*. Bob Dylan went electric, losing his die-hard folk fans without a backward glance. The Scott McKenzie song *San*

Francisco (Be sure to wear flowers in your hair) became an anthem for a new dawn.

There was an explosion of creativity in ideas – In 1969 Steve Jobs met Steve Wozniak and started a conversation about electronics that would change the world. Psychedelics weren't illegal, so the doors of perception were opened by Aldous Huxley and Carlos Castaneda. Dr. Timothy Leary urged his followers to "tune in, turn on and drop out" of a conventional, rule based life. Joseph Campbell encouraged everyone to "Follow your bliss".

This was all pretty fascinating stuff to a girl at a convent school in Liverpool. I dreamt of running away but I was scared of the propaganda coming from the old world – the statistics of drug casualties, the lack of any kind of hopeful future to those without any education or track record of obedience. So I compromised. I followed the rules with a very bad attitude and I broke them whenever possible.

It was on such a day that I found myself skulking in a dark corridor outside the classroom (the nuns would never waste electricity). I was trying to think of a plausible excuse for being late... again. I was already on a warning for the crimes of "lying" (being economical with the truth) and "stealing" (borrowing a bicycle without asking). The thought of walking into class filled me with dread. I hated maths. It occurred to me that I could skip the whole lesson. If I was already in trouble for being late, I might as well be really late. This meant finding somewhere to hide for an hour.

At the end of the corridor was a door that led to the nun's quarters. We weren't allowed in, which made it all the more interesting. Later on in life I discovered that "the forbidden" is a trump card in any game of freedom. It allows you to feel free for a brief moment, but this is followed by long and dire consequences.

There are no short cuts to real freedom.

I knew there was a private chapel in the Nun's quarters, and as they would all be teaching, this was a perfect opportunity to see it, and a good place to hide until the next bell. Quietly opening the door I tiptoed along an even darker corridor to the chapel, sat down in one of the pews, and gazed up at a life sized statue of the crucifixion.

The image of the crucifixion had always compelled me because of the sheer intensity of it.

Intensity is the opposite of boredom, and boredom is something I struggled with. I was trapped in a world of rules, regulations, timetables and times tables. A world of deferred gratification – work hard, be happy later. A world that interpreted the life of Jesus, as the Hero's Journey on steroids. Compared to him we were spineless humans who should feel guilty. To emulate him we should suffer.

Looking at the blood stained body in front of me, I couldn't help wondering how many of his words had been misunderstood. If Jesus were here now what would he say? Perhaps something like "I over estimated your level of consciousness. Let me send a black monolith to get you up to speed before I arrive."

I could sense an important message coming from the statue in front of me. Perhaps I had been praying without realising, and now the answer was coming.

I leant forward to listen.

The sound of a door creaking.

The heavy footsteps of sensible shoes.

"Headmistress's office. NOW."

Being suspended from school is one way of being free, but it comes with complications. It was always presumed that I'd go to university and get a job as a teacher. Academic failure messed up that plan.

I had no qualifications, way too many opinions and an abiding passion for rock and roll music, pre-Raphaelite art and the stories of Camelot. Perhaps, with these, I could carve out some kind of future.

It was the summer of '69.

The era of optimism.

I left home in search of freedom.

CHAPTER 2

Just kids

I made my way to London, just like Dick Whittington, but without the cat.

Unlike Dick, I wasn't seeking fame and fortune, I was trading a conventional life, for one that felt free. Being young and naive, this meant the IDENTITY of freedom... Afghan coats, beads, patchouli oil, and pavement skimming trousers. These cost money, which meant I had to find a job pretty quickly.

I didn't want to do a boring job (clearly ahead of my time with the "do what you love" concept) so I turned to my three passions...

Pre-Raphaelite art drew a blank. Traditional art galleries paid badly and had a strict dress code. The stories of Camelot didn't fare much better. There were no positions at the local job centre for knights, poets or magicians. I couldn't teach mythology, because I'd left school without any qualifications.

This left rock and roll.

Wandering into Chrysalis Records (having been attracted to the butterfly logo on the door... transformation!) I asked for a job. These were the days, when you could just do things like that. Human Resources hadn't been invented yet, so there was just one Personnel Manager, who was responsible for everything, from hiring and firing to ordering the paper towels. He was somewhat distracted as he handed me an application form to fill in.

It turned out that my convent education wasn't completely wasted after all. I was apparently really good at punctuation and was also a very convincing liar. He hired me on the spot.

Reporting for work on Monday morning, I was immediately hit by a bout of imposter syndrome, so kept a low profile. No job was too menial if it meant I wasn't bored... filing, typing, collecting dry cleaning, making cups of tea. I was first in and last out (mainly because I had nowhere to live and the office was warm with a very nice sofa.)

I re-invented myself as one of the heroines in 9 to 5. Not Dolly Parton or Jane Fonda... possibly Lily Tomlin. I knew more about the way things worked than my boss did (though to be fair he was usually coping with some sort of hangover or shouting alpha male stuff into the telephone.) I also knew more than the secretaries (though this wasn't difficult as most of them had taken the job in order to meet pop stars, so work wasn't high on their agenda.)

Pretty soon I got promoted. And after that I got to do what I really, really wanted, which was to go on the road with rock and roll bands. This was freedom with a capital F. Acting out the story of Peter Pan and the lost boys... refusing to grow up; living on a tour bus; fighting the Captain Hooks of the Corporate World (aka The Man).

Of course I wasn't actually free – in the same way that Wendy wasn't able to take full advantage of Neverland. That's how it was in those days. Boys could break rules and be adventurous, but girls needed to be sensible and manage the chaos, which was the by-product of all that creativity.

When I started out, I had a small rucksack, containing essential supplies of things like aspirin and chocolate biscuits – things to alleviate physical or emotional pain. I ended up with a flight case containing power leads, adaptors, cocaine, valium, gaffa tape, cigarettes, stapler guns, gothic candelabras, alcohol and a black book containing phone numbers for technicians, piano tuners, generators, dry ice, dodgy doctors, truck drivers and solutions to every problem.

There's a lot of romance around "the road" and a lot of stories that capture and perpetuate that romance. Cowboys in the Wild West. Hobos riding boxcars. Gypsies in painted caravans. These characters share common traits – a refusal to settle down in one place; a love of stories around campfires; music and alcohol; one night stands.

In short, these people were different, which was the opposite of boring. They were free.

Jack Kerouac wrote about them.

"The only people for me are the mad ones, the ones who are mad to live, mad to talk, mad to be saved, desirous of everything at the same time, the ones who never yawn or say a commonplace thing...".

In his "Summer of Love" bestselling book *On the Road*, Jack Kerouac conflated travelling people with interesting people, which led to quite the mythology!

Nowadays gap year kids go travelling as a rite of passage. They will describe their experience to future employers as "character building" or "humbling". But deep down they know (as we all knew back then) that it was far more to do with delaying the process of growing up, as long as possible.

Jackson Browne summed up life on the road more accurately.

"And when you stop to let 'em know, you've got it down, it's just another town along the road."

In his "Summer of Love" bestselling album *Running on Empty,* he captured the loneliness of late nights, loading trucks and sleeping solo. Romance is an identity, something manufactured, but it *feels* like an energy, so it kind of hovers mid way between the visible and invisible world... like dust.

Magic dust can create a spell that works for a little while, but it eventually wears off.

While under the spell, musicians could remain in a state of extended childhood. They were able to play all day without rules, just like the lost boys in Peter Pan or the inhabitants of Pleasure Island in Pinocchio. They could consume all the drugs and alcohol they liked, sleep until noon, eat unhealthy food, have sex with a different partner every night.

But of course there was a price to pay.

Unscrupulous businessmen (aka The Man) took full advantage of the fact that musicians hated grown up stuff, like contracts and royalties. I worked for Eric Burdon, who related toe curling stories of the way he, and his friend Jimi Hendrix, had been completely shafted.

While they were smoking weed, dropping acid and playing sold out shows, their manager, Mike Jeffery stole ALL the money. This was not an uncommon occurrence in the music business. "I'm putting it in a tax haven in the Bahamas" seemed a reasonable suggestion to people who sang...

"I go to parties, sometimes until four. It's hard to leave when you can't find the door."

"The paperwork is so complicated, you don't want to bother with it," Mike said. There is some truth in this. I find it hard to deal with tax returns and I'm not even stoned.

Mike Jeffery had a fear of flying (something neither Eric or Jimi were concerned about, as they were flying most of the time... albeit in another dimension). Because of this fear, he adopted the strange habit of double or triple booking each journey he had to take. By deciding at the last possible moment which flight to take, he thought he could outwit the universe.

In a bizarre twist of fate, Mike Jeffery died in a plane crash... or did he? When Eric went to the Bahamas to claim the millions of dollars he had earned, he found out that the holding company didn't exist. And neither did the money.

So, the Summer of Love... what went wrong?

On a metaphysical level, we realized that everything was energy and the vibration of peace and love was infinitely preferable to that of fear and war. We realized we were connected, so excluding groups of people based on race, gender or sexual orientation was ridiculous. We realized that the by-product of living without fear and judgment was massive amounts of creativity!

On the other hand, without an upgrade to our own energy system, most of these new ideas remained at the conceptual level. They were in our mind, not our body. We had enlightened minds and undisciplined bodies. We loved the identity of things, not their essence. We wanted things that *looked* cool, creative and beautiful. We wanted a hero that looked like Jesus, not acted like Jesus, and Jim Morrison fit that role perfectly... an adorable, wayward, creative child who refused to grow up.

"Unless you become as little children, you cannot enter the Kingdom of Heaven" was a favourite metaphor of Jesus. This has been interpreted in all manner of ways. What I think he meant was...

1　Children are imaginative which means they can play creatively. Creativity is a good thing as it solves problems, invents things and has the potential to make the world a better place for everyone.

2　Children live "in the now". When they play, they lose track of time, so in effect they're like little Zen Buddhist monks.

3　Children don't worry... meaning they don't spend a lot of time and energy being fearful about the future or regretting the past. Both of these are a waste of time, because we can't control the future and we can't change the past.

The way the phrase *"become as little children"* was interpreted by The Man (Church, Corporations and Government).

"Stay innocent and naive. We'll take care of everything – in exchange for a percentage of what you earn. You can't handle devils and demons, so leave it to us professionals."

The way *"become as little children"* was interpreted during the Summer of Love...

"I'm really special so I don't need to be disciplined. If there's a Kingdom of Heaven I want an access all areas pass NOW. Which pill do I swallow?"

This of course, is the response of self-indulgent children.

Perhaps if Jesus had added the word "healthy" or "conscious" in front of the word "children", things would have turned out a bit better.

CHAPTER 3

And they say that a hero will save us

Muriel Rukeyser was an American poet and activist, best known for her poems about equality, feminism and social justice. She said "the world isn't made of atoms, it's made of stories."

If the world is made of stories, then it's important to establish the main story that humanity has been driven by for thousands of years – the Hero's Journey. Some part of us yearns to know who we really are, and what we're really capable of. The Hero's Journey maps this quest. The Greeks had Odysseus. The Romans had Marcus Aurelius. The English had King Arthur. There are lots of versions of Arthur's story, so I'll just do a quick summary.

During The Dark Ages, England was engaged in endless civil wars. This meant it was difficult to grow crops or raise a family. Land was plundered. Nobody was safe. People lived in constant fear and poverty.

King Uther Pendragon wanted to sleep with the Lady Igraine, wife of his enemy Gorlois. To achieve this aim, he enlisted the services of

Merlin, a powerful sorcerer. Merlin transformed Uther into Gorlois so that he could trick Igraine into having sex with him.

Igraine became pregnant, and when the child, named Arthur, was born, Merlin took him away to be raised in secret. Obviously he was a little bit magical as he was conceived through magic. He was to be "the once and future King" who would unite all of England.

At the appointed time, Arthur revealed his credentials as the true King, by pulling a sword from a stone. The sword was called Excalibur. It was also a bit magical and very powerful. With it Arthur fought many battles. His fame spread and soon knights came from far and wide to fight under his banner – including the most famous, most handsome knight of all... Lancelot.

Nobility, honour and values came back into being. Arthur, Lancelot and the other knights sat at a round table to signify equality rather than the hierarchies of old. Arthur righted many wrongs and brought law and order to the land. England was now a more peaceful and prosperous place to live.

Every woman in the land wanted to marry Arthur, so when it came to getting wed, he obviously chose the most beautiful – the young and innocent Guinevere. Just a child really. And we know what happens to them, once the summer of love comes around.

Guinevere's appearance at court completed the fairytale. Camelot was born. A place of beauty, culture and above all... balance. Music, dancing and art merged with jousting competitions, avenging injustice and law making. This was a true marriage of masculine and feminine values.

The idea of romance came into being. Prior to this, romance wasn't really a thing. Marriages were arranged – to enhance the power of two families, to stop tribes from killing each other, or to produce children who could work on the farm. The knights introduced chivalry, or love from a distance. They wrote poetry, sang love songs and rescued damsels from towers.

One damsel who didn't fare well in the Camelot story was the Lady of Shalott. We don't know who cast a spell on her, but she was trapped in a tower on an island in the river, near Camelot. The spell dictated that she only view the outside world through a mirror. If she looked directly through the window, she would die. And so she sat at her loom, weaving whatever images she could see in the glass.

Imagine how boring that would be... under a spell, having to sit all day making tapestries depicting life on the outside. Of course, though we think her story is a ridiculous myth from ancient times, how many of us stare at the screen of a smart phone, trapped by the spells of The Man, while we scroll through the lives of other people. Just a thought...

Camelot merged the old religion of Paganism (energy) with the new religion of Christianity (rules). This wasn't the version of Christianity Jesus taught, because by this time his words had been mangled beyond recognition.

Geometry Warzone – The True Cross versus The Circle of Life

Arthur's half sister Morgan le Fay was a Pagan – someone who believed in the power of nature, where all things (animals, plants and Gods) have a masculine and feminine component.

Arthur was a Christian, someone who believed in the Holy Trinity of Gods – Father, Son and Holy Spirit. All three points of this triangle are masculine. (Red flag number one).

For a while there was balance between Arthur and his sister Morgan le Fay. She had her rituals. He had his rules. One of the many rules Arthur created, was the one in which treason was a non-pardonable offence. (Red flag number two – Jesus forgave everyone).

Everything in Camelot was going so well... until of course Guinevere fell in love with Lancelot. To be fair, everyone was in love with Lancelot. Morgan le Fay, all the ladies at court, even Arthur (bromance). One can only imagine the force of energy Guinevere struggled with for maybe ten minutes, maybe ten years – who knows? Anyway, she slept with him.

This caused a massive problem for Arthur. He couldn't pardon them, because both Lancelot and Guinevere had committed a non-pardonable offence. So his patriarchal law making, ensured that he lost both his best friend (who roamed around in misery for the rest of his life) and his wife (who entered the convent for the rest of her life).

The world lost its balance and became very masculine. Arthur and his knights meanwhile, became obsessed with finding The Holy Grail. However, because they only believed in the physical world, they thought the Grail was an actual cup – the one Jesus used during The Last Supper. Just like the fishermen, knights didn't understand metaphors.

Christians are told that the Holy Trinity is a "three in one" God. God the Father, God the Son and God the Holy Spirit are all separate, yet they are one being. This makes no sense in the physical world, where things can't be separate and part of a whole at the same time.

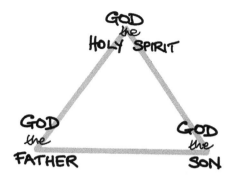

Not so holy trinity, more a patriarchal triangle

The Trinity does makes sense in the energy world. Viewed through the lens of energy, God the Father would represent masculine energy (strategic and rule based). Jesus, the Son, would represent feminine energy (forgiving and compassionate). The Holy Spirit would be the creative possibilities that emerge when masculine and feminine energy come into balance (1+1 = 3).

Meanwhile, back in Camelot, what became of the Lady of Shalott? She was sitting at her loom one day minding her own business, when Lancelot rode by on a horse.

Does my ego look big in this?

27

She couldn't help herself. She left the loom and rushed to gaze directly at his face.

*The mirror cracked from side to side; "the curse
is come upon me," cried the Lady of Shalott.*

She got in a boat and floated downstream. By the time she reached Camelot, she was dead.

The Camelot story compels us because it reveals so much about the human condition.

On the plus side...

1   The desire to be a hero. To prove our worth, like Arthur.
2   To be as cool and charismatic as Lancelot.
3   To be as powerful and magical as Morgan and Merlin.
4   The possibility of building a utopian society... heaven on earth.

On the minus side...

1   How seduced we are by the identities of both heroism and magic, when in reality, both require huge amounts of discipline.
2   How powerless we are when hit by the high voltage energy of desire.
3   How attached we are to taking sides. Was Arthur wrong in his decision? Was Guinevere a slut or an innocent victim? Was Lancelot a player or hopelessly in love? Was the Lady of Shallot a damsel or a sorceress? Was Morgan le Fay a High Priestess or a wicked witch?
4   The possibility of creating a dystopian society... hell on earth.

If we want to move towards the metaphysical world, we need to sort out our relationship to energy. We have to place less importance on the way things look on the surface, and develop the intuition to perceive what's really going on.

But for now let's go back to this story, where the Summer of Love is over, the hippies have dispersed and the music has changed its tune.

CHAPTER 4

Machine Head

I had now progressed to working for heavy metal bands. Metal was angry music. Perhaps it was a masculine rebellion to the sentiments of peace and love that went before it, or perhaps it arose from disillusionment. For the majority of young people, life hadn't changed since the Summer of Love. Heavy metal lyrics were dark and depressing, partly misogynistic and partly 19th century romantic. Women were objectified as Sluts or Faery Queens.

If rock and roll music was associated with the child, in particular the flower child, then heavy metal was more about no-holds-barred teenage fantasy. Massive lighting rigs. Enormous stage sets. Towering P.A. Stacks. Extravagant Pyrotechnics. Everything had to be BIG to create spectacle, and above all everything had to be LOUD

Heavy metal bands epitomized the male archetypes of the Camelot story. There was always a sensible member of the band (Arthur) who was good with numbers and made things happen by being the amenable liaison between the band and everyone else. There was the hot one (Lancelot) who attracted all the groupies and there was the crazy one (Merlin) who was completely unpredictable and super creative, so forgiven various excesses.

In the band, Arthur and Lancelot would compete for the Guineveres of the day, who were fey and winsome, with long hair and floaty skirts made of silk handkerchiefs. The road crew of heavy metal bands behaved like marauding knights, emulating their heroes while pledging absolute loyalty to the King.

Sometimes the three main archetypes of Arthur, Lancelot and Merlin were at war with each other, which meant an awful lot of drama on the road. By this time I was working for Ritchie Blackmore (Merlin). Nowhere was rivalry more apparent than in the relationship between Ritchie and whoever his Lancelot lead singer was at the time (none of them lasted more than a couple of tours).

Ritchie Blackmore's guitar playing has been described as "genius" and like many talented people, he felt the need to erect a barricade between himself and the "normal" world. For this reason he developed strange idiosyncrasies, which did the job nicely. He wouldn't stay in the usual hotels, so we had to find haunted houses or gothic manors within driving distance of each gig. He would only wear black clothes, had to have black candles in his dressing room (hence the gothic candelabra in my Mary Poppins bag) and he would only drink Johnny Walker black label.

Ritchie's love of the paranormal was shared by another guitar hero, Jimmy Page. Jimmy was obsessed with Aleister Crowley and the occult. Heavy metal became associated with fantasy worlds – witches, wizards, demons, darkness, faery queens and magical kingdoms. Two of its biggest anthems were Led Zeppelin's *Stairway to Heaven* and AC/DC's *Highway to Hell*, which pretty much covers the whole spectrum.

THE STEREO MONOLITHS

**Though impressive, touching these monoliths
didn't lead to species upgrade, just tinnitus**

Productions became bigger as each band competed to lay claim to the greatest level of excess. The road crew on these tours had a real hero's story going on. Their claim to fame was endurance. They took pride in the fact that they could work all night without the need for sleep or food; they could get around any technical challenge, playing Tetris with black boxes to fit an oversized P.A. onto a stage that was way too small; creating a cat's cradle of chain hoists to hang a lighting rig from a roof that was far too weak to hold its weight.

They were unstoppable. When Cozy Powell's drum riser wouldn't fit through the corridors of a hundred year old theatre, they took sledge-hammers, knocked a hole in the wall, then had it rebuilt after the show. When someone left a car, parked where the truck needed to be, they levered it into a swimming pool, destroying both car and pool. When the manager presented a bill (oil slicks are expensive to clean up) they ceremoniously burnt it.

Road crew stories became legend, all revolving around the same themes...

1   Excessive drug and alcohol consumption and a cavalier attitude to sex.

2   Ridiculing and breaking the rules that conventional society had to live by.

3   Superhuman endurance and cleverness – giving The Man the finger.

Because this was a very macho world, there was a lot of jargon. This made things a bit bewildering for me. Production meetings became more stressful, as I had to speed write terminology, acronyms and roadie slang, so that I could find out what they meant later. Obviously it's not a good idea to say "What does that mean?" in a boy's club as this would result in eye rolling and questions like "Whose idea was it to put a chick on the road anyway?"

Once the jargon was understood it was just a load of organisation, and ticking things off long to do lists. By this time I had created the flight case containing "everything you might need to cover every eventuality" so this helped. Also, when I was born, the three fairies hovering above my crib gave me the gifts of irony, stamina and common sense. I would have preferred the more traditional presents of incomparable beauty, goodness and a lovely singing voice... but not all stories are written by Disney.

I learnt to endure the cold of early load ins and the exhaustion of late load outs. I learnt how to be popular (FYI, just notice what makes people angry or upset.) In the macho world, if you can pre-empt an emotional response, and cut it off at the pass, people think you're a bit magical. It wasn't real magic, but for now, I felt like I was winning the game of "finding freedom in a cool career." Other people seemed to be impressed by it. In social gatherings I would wait with secret superiority for the "And what do you do?" question.

Rock and roll made things happen without persuading or pleading, which felt a bit like spell-casting. I once asked the manager of a shop if he could stay open an hour past closing time, to sell Wellington boots. It was raining and the crew were sinking in mud.

"No" came the obvious first answer.

"It's for Deep Purple".

"How many pairs do you want?" came the second one.

Of course there was a flip side to this kind of God like power – narcissism. This is the shadow side of the Hero's Journey. There may be relentless focus and determination, but if the energy isn't coming from a good place, it can be destructive. A heavy metal tour could pass through a town like a hurricane, leaving devastation in its wake – angry venue managers, large invoices and weeping women.

The other problem was identity. Lots of things go wrong on the road. Fixing them intuitively or spontaneously unleashes a kind of "can do" energy, which makes us feel invincible and powerful. This energy doesn't come from us, it comes through us – that's how intuition and spontaneity work. But we want to own the power, so we create an identity around it.

The identity resembles Clint Eastwood in any of his spaghetti westerns. A lone cowboy who looks down at the small mindedness, fear and limitations of the "little people". He needs nothing and nobody... just a fast horse and a gun. He has no long-term partner or family because he doesn't want to be answerable to anyone else's needs. He's a lone wolf with cool buddies who he meets up with whenever he checks into town.

The philosophy of "don't ask for permission, ask for forgiveness" was rife with young guns in the music business. It made things happen that couldn't be achieved using more "normal" methods. Now that they're older, these knights of the road look back on these days with misty eyes. They ridicule box tickers and safety measures. They think the modern world lacks bravery, balls and big ideas.

When the techie geeks eventually picked up the baton, and Mark Zuckerberg coined the term "move fast and break things" – from behind the safety of a glass screen and an ergonomic chair...

They just rolled their eyes.

CHAPTER 5

I am an anarchist

And then came punk.

The music of the Summer of Love was all about the heart – sentimental and romantic. The music that followed it (heavy metal and progressive rock) was all about the head – complex arrangements, virtuoso performances and concept albums. In this territory, Pink Floyd reigned supreme. But there's a downside to living in the head... disconnection. It feels *Comfortably Numb*.

And so, things came crashing down to the gut, as Punk emerged.

Punk was the antithesis of progressive rock music. At first it wasn't music at all, just a lot of incomprehensible shouting. Musical proficiency wasn't a requirement (one chord was enough). Punk was like a delinquent child banging relentlessly on a drum.

The audience for punk responded in similar fashion... arms clamped firmly to their sides, jumping up and down, as if on pogo sticks, while spitting. It was quite a sight, though thoroughly miserable for the road crew. Sometimes the amps were so covered in phlegm that they slipped from their hands while trying to load the trucks.

Punk was more aligned to Paganism than Christianity. It wasn't spiritual, but the strange dancing, wild staring eyes and ritual vomiting certainly gave it a shamanic feel.

Some of the antisocial behaviours that surrounded the punk movement, were due to a change in the drug culture – from LSD to amphetamine sulphate. While LSD created a euphoric, loving state, amphetamines created focused rage and chronic insomnia.

Now that bands had wised up and were a bit more savvy about contracts and signatures, the gravy train of the Summer of Love had dried up. Business managers were forced to become more inventive.

They did so by embracing P.R.

Getting press for the band you represented, was like getting free advertising, and now that marketing had been infiltrated by Mad Men, who were stars in their own right, advertising had become very expensive.

For instance, the average spend for a Pink Floyd album cover was so outrageous that Storm Thorgerson, their art director, dared not even speak its name. On one photo-shoot he ordered 750 NHS hospital beds – all made up with sheets and blankets – and lined them up on a beach in the UK, along with a French maid and some random dogs.

It began to rain (obviously as this was England) so the beds had to be dismantled and stored somewhere. When asked if he got the shot, Storm merely said "No. Because I couldn't see the beds." Eventually the weather got better and they did it all over again. Ironically, the album was called *A Momentary Lapse of Reason.*

Against this backdrop of high art and unlimited budgets came the punk movement which was literally held together by safety pins... and fury.

The management scene was dominated by Malcolm McLaren, Jake Riviera and Dave Robinson.

Jake and Dave formed STIFF Records and quickly signed The Damned, Siouxsie and the Banshees and Ian Dury and the Blockheads. They made up for their lack of money with creative campaigns, like swapping the regular tour bus for a train. They embraced limitation by proudly proclaiming "Lo-Fi production!" They distributed free stickers that ended up on school satchels everywhere "If it ain't STIFF, it ain't worth a fuck."

But the Svengali of the day was Malcolm. He was looking for a front-man for a band, and when a skinny boy called John Lydon walked into the Kings Road shop he shared with Vivienne Westwood, he knew he'd found one. John (renamed Johnny Rotten) was wearing a *"I hate Pink Floyd"* T-shirt. He'd hand written the "I hate" part above the logo, and scratched holes through the eyes.

Malcolm didn't even need to know if he had any musical talent. He had a "look" that could be turned into an identity.

The Sex Pistols produced very few records but massive amounts of publicity. Malcolm encouraged the band to be rude and obnoxious and they complied. They sneered instead of smiled. They walked into meetings and put their feet up on coffee tables. They swore constantly, got drunk and vomited at every opportunity.

Eventually everything got completely out of hand and the band broke up. Malcolm moved onto another project – managing the career of a 13 year old Burmese girl, Annabella Lwin. Whereas Johnny Rotten was discovered in a clothes shop, Annabella was discovered in a dry cleaners where she had a Saturday job. Malcolm put together a backing band, and Bow Wow Wow was formed. Neither the X Factor, or The Voice had been invented, so the route to stardom was fairly random in those days.

I worked with Malcolm on the debut London gig of Bow Wow Wow at the Rainbow Theatre in Finsbury Park. Malcolm's plans for the show were of course completely over the top. He wanted all the seats removed to make way for fairground attractions, animals and dodgem cars. He wanted a huge helter skelter, down which Annabella would descend onto the stage.

Malcolm arrived at the first production meeting looking like an inscrutable Chinese Emperor. As the Health and Safety officer turned down each request, he remained impassive. He was listening, cat like, waiting for an opportunity. I knew it wouldn't end well, and was mentally working out the cancellation costs. Posters had been printed, tickets had been sold, deposits paid.

Once the Health and Safety officers had finished their summing up, Malcolm pounced.

"Public" he said, maintaining eye contact.

They looked confused.

"You keep saying we can't do this at a public gig."

"Well yes, we're only acting on their behalf. We have to consider their safety."

"So what if it's private?"

The officers looked at each other, trying to figure out where the conversation was leading.

"Well, obviously, we have no way of commenting on a private event."

Malcolm smiled, "In that case we are cancelling the show..."

The officers looked relieved.

"And we are replacing it with the Inauguration of the Bow Wow Wow fan club." Malcolm continued. "Cost of fan club membership, just happens to be the same cost of the current ticket price. Tickets already bought can be swapped for membership cards on the evening by our security staff. Good day gentlemen."

The gig went ahead. Nobody died.

This was a pivotal moment for me... witnessing Creative Energy upstaging rules in an elegant way. I was more familiar with Destructive Energy upstaging rules in an angry or narcissistic way. An "us" versus "them" face off.

Looking back I suppose this was my first encounter with the "both/ and" approach to problems. Everyone in the meeting was focused on an either/or outcome – either the gig would go ahead in a vastly compromised form, or it would be cancelled. Malcolm's "pause" was him waiting for the both/and to arrive.

Music has always brought a sense of freedom – or at least respite from the ordinary world. When music became too clever and sophisticated, it excluded a lot of kids. They felt bored and resentful, so they wanted intensity to counteract the dullness. They wanted to find expression for their anger, disconnection and loneliness... the "lost in space" feeling that David Bowie had captured in Space Oddity.

Here am I floating in my tin can, far from the world...

It was this loneliness that I tapped into at the end of the Knebworth Rock festival. I was cold, wet and had hardly slept in days. Standing on the stage, I gazed down at what looked like the aftermath of a battle, illuminated by little bonfires... the fans were so cold they'd torn off all the toilet doors and set fire to them. Kids were sleeping in bin liners.

The incessant rain had led to poor ticket sales so the promoter had lost money. He had borrowed from Don Murfet, generally described as the man behind The Man... I mean how much testosterone do you need? A whoop of helicopter blades signaled Don's arrival with an empty suitcase. The horror! The horror! There was no money.

Being a knight of the road is exciting for a while, but it's exhausting. I was tired of the endless endurance test and the fierce independence. Even the highly charged war stories had lost their charm. I wanted to experience the romantic side of Lancelot. The poetry, not the fight. The civility of the court, not the mud of the battle ground.

As the era of the New Romantics dawned, my passion for pre-Raphaelite art was re-kindled.

Perhaps it was possible to find freedom in love.

SECTION ONE CONCLUSIONS

Identity

As a child we are taught that validation comes from working hard – first at school, later in a career. Work is how we create our identity. The saying "Make a name for yourself" literally sums this up. "What do you do?" is one of the first questions we ask a stranger, because it's the primary way we determine the identity of another.

However, it's not the identity of work that's important, it's the type of energy we use to drive it. Work is great if it's driven by the challenge to solve shared problems or the desire to become competent. This brings camaraderie, jokes and joy. Unfortunately, for many of us, it's driven by fear. We know our identity is fragile and could crack at any minute revealing the incompetent child we still believe we are on the inside.

Instead of transforming our energy, we build up our identity. This creates two problems. First we have to keep proving ourselves to the outside world, which is exhausting. Second, all positive feedback for our performance goes to the identity, not to ourselves, so it doesn't sustain us. Underneath the identity, we still feel inadequate, fraudulent or scared.

Choice

We still believe in the old idea that careers require the masculine attributes of single-minded focus and independence, not the feminine attributes of co-operation and inclusivity. Throughout history, women weren't allowed into the work arena, so the identity of the solo male genius got propagated.

Many women dealt with this bias by suppressing their feminine attributes and adopting masculine ones, in order to be allowed into the boy's club. As the "lost" boy's club was led by Peter Pan, the roles available to women were either Wendy (mother of the boys) or Tinker Bell (one of the boys) ... colluding with, or indulging childish male behaviour.

In the energy world, creativity and child like perception go hand in hand because "seeing things with new eyes" is essential to the creative process. Child like behaviour is part of the identity world, so is a different thing entirely.

Story

The Hero's journey has an upside and a downside. Having a direction of travel is a good thing, as is having the discipline to overcome obstacles on the path. However the subtext is that the journey is linear – we can't enjoy life unless we have endured something difficult first.

This creates the twisted logic of believing we have to "deserve" happiness, as a prize for suffering *"I've paid my dues"*. We feel we have to justify taking a holiday, because *"I've just been working SO hard lately I need a break"*. We're embarrassed to be seen doing nothing *"I'm currently between jobs, but I'm incredibly busy!"* These ideas are not conducive to pausing and becoming more aligned to our inner creativity. They just create a lot of drama and noise.

In the energy world we are superhuman, which means we have the capacity inside us to go "beyond human". When this truth is interpreted through the identity world, super human means better than other humans. This makes us competitive, tough and obsessed with winning.

On the plus side, the bonding I experienced during life on the road was intense. It's been likened to the bonding that occurs in times of war. We lose our individual identities because if we don't pull together as a team, the impossible wouldn't happen. To this day the description "He's so rock and roll" is shorthand for being indomitable, creative and edgy. Unfortunately, like everything, it's the identity that's lingered rather than the spirit of it.

SECTION TWO

Looking for Freedom in Love

CHAPTER 6

The future is feminine

I had a boyfriend. During my time in heavy metal, he was the one who patiently explained all that technical jargon. We sat in pizza restaurants while he covered paper napkins with drawings of lighting rigs and electrical grids. He had no interest in macho, misogynistic behaviour, but was kind and soulful. He was more like Percival, King Arthur's honourable knight.

Leaving rock and roll meant I could now spend more time with him. I looked forward to the domestic comfort I'd denied myself for so long... the familiarity of sleeping in the same bed each night, waking up without wondering where I was and what new problems the day would bring.

But first I needed a job, or a "real" job as my father would call it. Breaking into the corporate world in the 1990s was a bit different to joining the music business. Managers were less maverick and more grown up in their approach to work. They were looking for people with qualifications, resumes, C.V.s and other pieces of paper containing WORDS.

They also seemed to have a lot more fear – which is probably why they needed all that paper. Having pieces of paper gave them the security of knowing they had done their job correctly. They had tangible proof that they had employed the right person. Therefore they could be absolved of any blame if things went wrong in the future. Humiliation is horrible energy and needs to be avoided at all costs.

Paperwork and processes slow down energy. This creates the illusion that the energy is actually being controlled, which can have disastrous consequences. For example...

One person has an idea (energy).

This idea needs to be approved by a team of people who each have different "box ticking" agendas (rules to make energy safe). "Will it work? Will it make me look good? Will everyone like it?"

It then needs to be signed off by finance. "Will it make money?"

This ends in "design by committee". Everyone is a little bit happy. Nobody is very happy. The final idea isn't as good as the original idea, which was quirky, exciting and different – these words usually mean "not safe" in the business world. The process of getting to an agreement often clashes with the need to meet a deadline, so either the idea can't be used, or a lot of money is wasted paying overtime or penalties.

Back in the 1990s, having an idea and offering to take the hit if it went wrong, was enough to get you a job without qualifications. Pretty soon I was working in a marketing company... safely ensconced behind a desk with a computer and a diary full of meetings.

The move from life on the road to the corporate world was a bit of a culture shock. Things happened slowly. There were lots of conversations between clients and suppliers. The clients were pernickety rather than demanding, focusing on tiny details and changing their mind a lot. The suppliers were expensive, because they didn't actually make anything themselves. They bought stuff from other suppliers and marked it up. Nobody went direct because that involved risk.

Everyone was smartly dressed, but even more disconcerting was the fact that they wore something different every day. I needed a new wardrobe. Shopping had never been a big thing for me, mainly because I started work before shops were open, finished after they closed, and spent a lot of time on a tour bus. This was about to change.

I set off, meandering through streets lined with expensive boutiques on my way to a cheap department store. Suddenly, a flash of dark orange caught my eye – a cardigan on a shop window mannequin. It was the perfect colour... quite close in shade to the red flag that accompanied it, when the owner of the boutique greeted me like a long lost relative.

First she admired my taste. Then, when I asked the price, she helped me try it on and told me how beautiful I looked in it. I was used to people calling me smart, not beautiful. "It's cashmere" she whispered when it was far too late to turn back. "And wait till you see how amazing it looks with this skirt, and..." As she bustled about the shop picking things off racks I peeked slyly at the price tag on the cardigan. For a moment, I couldn't breathe.

Eventually (being the only two people in the shop) an air of complicity was created between us. She was no longer a pushy sales woman. She was my Fairy Godmother, transforming me from bohemian road crew to glamorous business woman. This was a different kind of power. It was sexy and sophisticated. I didn't care about the money. I wanted this feeling of transformation to last forever.

We both looked at my reflection in the oval mirror. I was so high on the energy I didn't recognize myself. I imagined her saying "You shall go to the ball!" but instead, the words I heard were my own... "I shall buy it all!"

This was the beginning of my shopping addiction. The irony that I was now working in marketing was not lost on me. During the week I thought up campaigns to seduce people into buying things they didn't need. "Free gift with purchase!" At the weekend I was seduced by the same marketing I'd been compiling all week. It made no sense at all...

to my mind. But the impulse to buy wasn't coming from my mind, it was coming from a deeper place. I was under a spell. Like an alcoholic, I had to hide carrier bags from Percival, who would have thought I was insane. I spent more in one shopping trip than he spent in an entire year.

I began studying psychology and reading business books, partly to advance my career but perhaps hoping to understand my own behaviour. Before the Summer of Love, success in business was based on meeting a need. Nobody had much in the way of consumer goods, so things like televisions, refrigerators and cars were considered luxury items. Work took up most of men's lives, child rearing, housekeeping and cooking took up most of women's lives. Therefore, marketing focused on selling labour saving devices.

By the 1980s everything had changed. Far more people had the basic things they needed. If you were only in the business of selling solutions that met a need, this was a bit tricky. Business solved this problem… by inventing more needs. In order to do this, they went to the gap between the physical world and the metaphysical one…The magic dust (aka Brand Marketing).

Here's how the magic works…

To make a t-shirt you need materials and labour. The cost of these real things is for example $4. But if you put the name of someone famous on the t-shirt, its value is now $40. The extra $36 is called the "brand equity" which is just an IDEA in the mind of the consumer. It doesn't actually exist.

Brands create energy… an overwhelming desire for something you want. Love and creativity also create energy, but this energy is unpredictable and could result in either rejection or disappointment. Love and creativity are hard to control. Brands, on the other hand, can make you feel happy, sexy, superior or part of an exclusive club. Unfortunately these feelings don't last very long. This is bad news for consumers, but very good news for The Man.

All you need is trust, and a little bit of magic dust

Because we live in the either/or perception of reality, we have conflicts of interest. We want love and we want control. We want to win and we want to belong. This is why brands are so popular. Brands allow you to feel superior to others and also to fit in with the few people you might actually like... in other words controlled love, simultaneous winning and belonging.

On the metaphysical level, we have a blueprint for "becoming". Becoming more accomplished at something brings us joy. If we learn to dance or play the piano or communicate in a different language, our soul glows. We are becoming... becoming a dancer, becoming a musician, becoming fluent. This requires effort, so we're more likely to go for its counterpart in the identity realm... becoming cool, cute or sexy. This gives us an instant identity upgrade without any of the discipline.

Knowing this didn't help my shopping addiction – clothes, cosmetics, cocktails... my inner pre Raphaelite was having a lovely feminine time. Of course this was the identity of femininity, the brand, not the energy of it. My energy was still predominantly masculine.

I embraced the corporate world, like a calm port after a storm. The fact that I'd been forged in the heat of battle meant that by comparison, it wasn't too challenging. I got promoted. Now I had no reason to curb my enthusiasm for spending money, or my creative ideas... they were welcomed.

Many inmates of the corporate world were uncomfortable proposing ideas or making decisions. They were used to finishing work in time for dinner. They were familiar with the concept of eating dinner! They were scared of The Man.

I wasn't scared.

Which is why the evolutionary force stepped in with its *coup de grace*.

I fell in love with him.

CHAPTER 8

I am a woman in love

It's called falling in love for a reason. Nobody says "rising in love" as this would imply some skill in directing the energy.

I fell in love with my new boss. My old corporate boss lacked powers of persuasion, so was replaced with a more Svengali version. Brand marketing requires sales, and sales require some dexterity with the magic dust.

It started out in the manner of all romantic comedies... I didn't like him. I'd been able to run rings around his predecessor, so it felt like my power was being taken away. My new boss made it clear that he was definitely the one in control. I looked for opportunities to catch him out, so that I could re-assert my command of the situation. At home, I complained endlessly to Percival about his arrogance and the fact that he was outrageously overpaid. In the office, I colluded with colleagues and rolled my eyes when he made decisions without consulting anyone.

All his decisions paid off. He had some uncanny ability to know what would work, what would look good, what people would want... before they knew it themselves. He was supremely confident at making decisions. Clients loved him because they could piggyback on his creativity and claim it as their own. They would retell stories of brand-planning meetings, casting themselves in the role of maverick decision maker. "Yeah, we went out on a limb with this one, but you know I had this gut feeling and thought, fuck it, let's do this thing". Of course, in reality all the clients were indecisive scaredy-cats.

I started to soften my initial appraisal of him. He wasn't a narcissist, he was a creative genius. He reminded me of Malcolm McLaren... if Malcolm looked less like an elf and more like George Clooney. It was a devastating combination. As I softened, he started making his moves. Subtle ones at first, a look, a smile, a conspiratorial glance across the board room table. Something inside me ignited as if in agreement to the unspoken rules of a game about to be played out... ready player one. This ignited thing was not in my head, it was in my body.

When he made a move, I made one back. If he sent an ambiguous text, I would construct an equally ambiguous one back. I made my messages look witty, and off the cuff, whereas in reality I would compose, delete, recompose, delete, recompose... send. I wanted him to think I was clever and sexually confident. I didn't believe either, and would wait, nervously for his reply. When my phone pinged, I thought I would jump out of my body.

I got excited about going to work and started lying to Percival about my need to stay late in the office. *It's just flirting*, I reasoned with myself. *Nothing's going to happen. It's just an antidote to boredom... a fun game.* In any game, it's important to assess the skill level of your opponent. In my euphoric haze, I failed to do that. My boss had form to say the least. He would advance and flirt, then just as I was hooked, he'd retreat by being quiet or moody. Like a laboratory rat, I worked harder and harder to find the right lever to press, the one that made him gaze at me with admiration.

They say a gambling addiction works in the same way. Gamblers aren't addicted to winning at the roulette wheel, they're addicted to the moment just before the ball lands. In that moment a gap opens up containing two possible outcomes... black or red, win or lose. It's the delicious feeling of both/and, before the either/or option is finally revealed. It's a glimpse into the metaphysical world, before the ball lands, bringing us back to the fixed, final reality of the physical one.

Did my boss like me? Did he like me "in that way". The answer was clearly yes, but how much? Was it a "one-night stand" attraction or was this something deeper? Were we going to be an item? A creative partnership? A great love affair? I was hooked on the uncertainty. I wanted answers, but I also didn't want answers, in case they were the answers I didn't want to hear, and meanwhile, I just kept playing.

Sometimes a colleague would suggest I was working too hard without the necessary financial reward, but I brushed this off. My boss and I were in an exclusive club, two super humans achieving groundbreaking things together... unlike ordinary mortals. The colleague would offer to stay behind to help me "*No!! Please go!!* I kept any urgency out of my voice, but managing my inner state was becoming exhausting.

In my reasonable moments, I conceded they had a point and made a conscious effort to withdraw my energy from the game. That's when my boss turned up the heat, praising me in front of the client, saying he couldn't do it without me, making me feel special... loved... chosen. (Damn that Cinderella story in my sub conscious). He'd put his hand on my shoulder and leave it there a second too long, while I lost the ability to breathe.

Days turned into weeks. He would advance and retreat, like a skilled matador, playing, flirting, coaxing until I was too exhausted by my own desire to do anything but submit. I faced him, breathless, waiting for the sword to pierce my heart. Above all, wanting the need to end.

The sex of course was amazing... the kind of intense, passionate, out of body experience that happens after a build up like that. Now that the uncertainty of whether sex would happen or not was over, I hoped I'd be able to return to some sort of equilibrium. This didn't happen. The need to be with him just increased. The game continued, only now the stakes were higher.

I carried on living with Percival. Unlike my boss, he actually cared for me. I didn't want to hurt him, and I persuaded myself that what I was doing was just a fling. It wasn't even as grand as an affair. After all, people who have affairs go to hotels and have weekends away. They say things like "I love you more than life" or "I wish we could be together... if only I didn't have this mean wife/expensive mortgage/ crazy mother in the attic".

I didn't care that we weren't properly an item. I felt amazing. I was no longer a knight of the road, I was in love with a knight and not just any knight, I was in love with Lancelot, the most alpha knight of all. My transformation from geek to Guinevere was complete. Life felt magical.

The office meeting was no longer a series of boring conversations and check lists, it was a round table of harmony, humour and creativity.

New ideas tumbled over each other. Serendipities occurred. I let go of the need to control everything and experienced the flow of life.

We've been raised to believe that lust comes from our lower, animal nature and love comes from our upper, divine one. Religion interprets our animal instinct as the dark part of us that makes us do bad things.

In the metaphysical realm, the dark has no connotations of good/bad. The dark is just the part of us we keep hidden from ourselves. We don't hide our "bad" characteristics, the term "badass" is a mark of respect these days. Instead, we hide what we think is hideous and unforgiveable in us... namely our neediness and our vulnerability.

Sexual desire will bring that neediness and vulnerability to the surface in a way that a mutually supportive, loving relationship just can't do. Perhaps sex is a portal to the divine, providing a way for us to heal this shadow side of our nature.

Of course back then I didn't see this as a divinely orchestrated plan to help me feel and heal my repressed neediness. I didn't feel vulnerable... yet. I felt guilty, excited and out of control, in a good way. Sexual energy is way more powerful than the risk incurred by spending money. Unfortunately my shopping addiction wasn't cured by falling in love. If anything it got worse, because now there was... lingerie. Agent Provocateur and Victoria's Secret. I may have been in bondage gear, but at last I felt completely free. You know already this doesn't end well, so let's stay a while in the land of happy and explore some science.

When two people meet, they evaluate their identity, which is why magazines devote so much space to beauty and six packs. Once two people get into an intimate relationship, they meet in the energy world. Relationships are a crucible, like some kind of laboratory for energy mixing. At first things are harmonious, but when repressed needs come to the surface, they become turbulent.

WINNER: INDEPENDENCE & CHARISMA
LOSER: DEPENDENCE & NEEDINESS

Our natural response to turbulence is to pull back into independence. Unfortunately, it's too late for this now, because our energy has become entangled. Scientists have found that once the quantum particles of atoms have become entangled, they will always have an effect on each other – regardless of how far apart they are separated.

This is a bit of a mind fuck to people who think they can get away from a difficult relationship by going to another country, or burying it in their subconscious for a few years. Entangled particles exist outside of time and space. It's the baked in strategy of the universe, to try to get us to work out our differences.

But of course we're not playing ball. We still think the old strategy of "distancing" works, but put people in a highly charged situation... the office party with too much alcohol, a cinema showing a romantic comedy, or a power ballad at high volume... and feelings that were buried years ago can resurface freshly minted!

Why are we attracted to people who seem to have more power than us? Now that women (in the western world) are allowed to be independent, earn money and have rights over their own reproductive system, you would think the victim archetype would be consigned to history, so how come women swooned over *50 Shades of Grey*?

Surrendering into the flow is a metaphysical concept, in which we let go of our identity and allow the energy of the life force to direct us. This is not the same as surrendering to a crazy, controlling person with a helicopter and a set of handcuffs. That's the problem with mixing up the physical and metaphysical worlds.

When I fell in love with my boss, I felt like Guinevere, child like, romantic, flirty and irresponsible. When he reciprocated my love, I felt like Lancelot, in a bromance with Lancelot. We went on crusades together (client meetings up and down the country), achieved heroic tasks (creative campaigns) and laughed at the limitations of lesser human beings. We were golden.

However my time as Lancelot came to an end when the tables turned (it's easy for round tables to do this). Someone had to organize spreadsheets, budgets and timelines in order to make all the ideas happen. I ended up with less of the spontaneity and more of the responsibility.

Knights avoid responsibility. Kings are good at responsibility, but knights prefer winning competitions and opportunities for travel. When things become quiet at home, there's always a crusade going on somewhere overseas. Lancelot went to New York while I "held the fort". He was seducing a new crowd of admirers, while I was dealing with the fallout from the old ones. I was working harder than ever to keep everyone happy, but it was never enough because they wanted him, the identity of him, and I would only ever be second best.

As his power grew, mine diminished. Now I was out of control, but in a bad way. There was "a disturbance in the force". I became needy, suspicious and spellbound.

I had become the Lady of Shalott.

CHAPTER EIGHT

What fresh hell is this?

A wise rabbi once said that all our problems stem from using the wrong words. He was at a restaurant, where one of his fellow diners said "I love fish". The rabbi paused and said "Really? You catch the fish, you cook it and you eat it. Are these the actions of love? Now the fish is no more."

And so it is with people. We desire them. We think the love we are looking for is inside them. We think that if we catch them we will be able to hold onto the love. We think if we get married, that will act as some sort of guarantee... that the love will be locked down in the words of a marriage contract.

But the love isn't in the other person, or the piece of paper, it's in the energy of desire. It's in the gap between two people. We try to close the gap, and in the process of doing that, we often end up killing the love.

Most of what we call Love is actually Fish Love.

If we learnt to hold the tension in the gap we could experience metaphysical love, which is just... love. But we are unskilled at holding this energy. It's unfamiliar to us, so we either rush forward to cling, or we drop the tension, by withdrawing. If intimacy brings up feelings of neediness we'll cling and if it brings up feelings of suffocation, we'll withdraw. There's no right or wrong answer, it's just different sides of the same coin. Being a high achiever, I experienced both. I felt neediness with my boss and suffocation with my boyfriend.

People have been describing love for thousands of years. Love in the physical realm can be jealous, angry, possessive, romantic, sentimental and erotic. The Man is of course everywhere behind these scenarios, because wherever there are strong emotions, there's a big selling opportunity. New love, unrequited love, and love that's gone wrong can sell everything from teddy bears and chocolates to porn and sex toys, with boutique hotels somewhere in the middle.

"Mirrors on the ceiling, pink champagne on ice..."

St Valentine is the patron saint of love, but in reality he should be the patron saint of marketing. Valentines Day makes us believe that energy can be created by things – particularly if those things are either very expensive or very unique. No wonder some people give up on romantic love, and opt for loving Jesus instead. At least Jesus always loves you back no matter what you do. Also Jesus "saves" which is like catnip to the damsel, who lives to be rescued.

But what if, instead of loving by the old rules of win/lose, we learnt how to manage the energy of desire better?

The archetypes of the heart are the Knight and the Damsel and because energy doesn't have a gender, we have both patterns inside us. The Knight wants independence and the Damsel wants connection. The

Knight wants to possess, the Damsel wants to be possessed. The Knight wants to win, the Damsel wants to be rescued – usually from herself, but that's by the by.

Managing energy, means managing the tension in the gap between these two polarities. It's not a competition, it's a "both/and" dance.

We love the Knight archetype, because we love feeling charismatic and courageous. But we hate the flip side of this energy, which is neediness and vulnerability.

In a funny way, this makes evolution look like a wise parent...

God aka The Life Force: *"I'll give you something (Lancelot) so you get to experience high frequency energy, then I'll take it away, so you get to experience low frequency energy. (The Lady of Shallot). After all, you can't become good at managing energy until you experience the whole range. It's like learning to play the piano – you have to know what all the notes sound like before deciding which ones to play."*

How we COULD respond...

"Thanks God. Now I know where to place my focus, I can create some interesting music."

How we ACTUALLY respond when Lancelot leaves...

"OMFG I think I'm going to die. There's this terrible pounding in my ears".

God: *"That's you banging on those keys."*

Me: *"Make it stop, make it stop..."*

If enlightenment comes from *Living in the Now,* then the end of a relationship is about as far away from *Now* as you can get. It's the dark side of the moon. The first thing that kicks in is nostalgia (living in the past) then regret (living in the past) then fantasy (living in the future). BASICALLY ANYWHERE BUT NOW.

When I look back (nostalgia) I remember the excitement of anticipation. It was like being a child on Christmas Eve. I would catch Lancelot's eye, while he was holding court in a room full of people, and an electric current would run through me as if my spine was an earthing rod.

Energy is amazing when left to its own devices. Unfortunately we try to wrestle it to the ground and put it in a box where we can keep it under control. Once you start sleeping with someone, the old paradigm comes at you with a fury. You wonder where the relationship is going. You leave the "now" and start speculating about the future. The world of identity is linear. Things have to be going in a direction to some kind of destination. I knew this was crazy, because I was happy with the way things were. I was strong and independent (oh the pride that comes before the fall!) I was Queen of Freedom. But the identity world... holy fuck is it powerful.

When I look back (regret) I try to figure out how it happened. I was blissfully unaware of the Damsel pattern until it got activated. I went from kick ass to needy. I didn't want freedom, I wanted to have and to hold! I wanted to know where he was, what he was doing and who he was doing it with.

After regret, came fantasy. I imagined that I hadn't screwed things up by becoming needy... that there was another universe somewhere where we were still together (FYI reading up on the multiverse really is clutching at straws). I imagined him being knocked over by a bus and developing amnesia, completely forgetting my needy behaviour and only remembering my glory days. He would arrive in the office "Hey Babe... sorry am I late? Apparently I've been in hospital."

We're used to the concept that high vibration energy gets channeled through us. Musicians often say "I can't take ownership of this idea, it just came through." They attribute it to the Muse.

We're less familiar with the concept that low vibration energy also comes through us. Negative ideas are just a thought away. They're the black keys. They give nostalgia to joy; yearning to love; edge to drama. Music would have less of a range if we only had the white keys.

When we fall in love, the energy channels open, which feels wonderful while the good stuff is coming through. It's all light hearted bromance of witty asides, adventure and high jinx. But as soon as the lower frequencies arrive, it's every man for himself.

If we were more evolved, we would manage, and even transform the low vibration stuff. We are certainly capable of doing this, because we do it for children and pets. For instance, we can love a dog when it's needy or insecure (*she's so cute*). We can forgive anger (*he's just feeling threatened*) and greed (*he's a dog, that's what dogs do*). We even blame ourselves (*I shouldn't have left the sausages on the table*).

But when it comes to people, we are less forgiving of our low frequency nature. We pretend that we never have negative, needy or controlling thoughts. We pretend to be evolved or spiritual. It's very bewildering to discover that the tough, heroic person you thought you were, is actually just a well constructed identity, that can crack under pressure.

If we want to thrive in the energy world, we have to learn to balance. Too much independence makes us feels lonely and disconnected. Too much connection makes us feel trapped. We wobble to the left, then we course correct to the right. A little independence allows us to focus and get the job done. A little vulnerability allows us to do it in an open hearted way. Wobbling is good, because it means we're experiencing the whole spectrum.

Which is the only way we can develop some real skill... and learn to walk on the high wire.

CHAPTER 9

The tyranny of comparison

I figured out a few things during my time in marketing. Everything in the identity world has a value that we place on it, relative to the value that we place on ourselves. For convenience, the scale is 1-10.

If we see an amazing pair of shoes, we might put their value at 9. If we're feeling depressed, we might put our value at 4. Therefore the magnetic pull towards the pair of shoes is very strong.

If however we're feeling great and we score ourselves at an 8, and the shoes at 9, the pull is not very strong at all.

It's the job of marketing people to persuade us that we're actually a 4, and therefore definitely in need of the shoes "to get high" (now that good drugs are difficult to find).

As far as the purchase is concerned, this is a "no brainer", which means we don't even have to go into our head to do the math. It's obvious that we are getting more than we are giving. The shoes are giving us a feeling of invincibility and sexiness. They're only costing money (meh). Thus we can slam the credit card down with impunity.

The same principle (sadly) applies to relationships. If we assess ourselves as a 5 and we meet someone who is also 5, life is pleasant but there's no real energy pull.

If we meet someone we think is a 2, we put up a guard in case they drain our energy, because we find neediness so abhorrent.

If we meet someone who is a 9, there's a huge pull but we don't go towards it because we know they are out of our league. Even if something did happen, they would leave as soon as they realised we were a 5, and go looking for a higher number.

The exception to this rule is fantasy love – the kind we reserve for rock stars. Even though they are a 9, we can still love them... but from a distance. We could try to get closer, and sometimes we might actually meet them, in which case we become completely tongue-tied.

Working in the music business was a big eye opener for me, because of course once you get to know a 9, you usually find out they are a 5 after all. The difference between the 5 that they are, and the 9 you perceive them to be, is the brand equity, which as we know from a previous chapter, is a kind of made up thing.

So back to more normal relationships. If we're a 5, we look for a 7. This feels like a valuable exchange because we are gaining something – they are more smart, hot and charismatic than we are. This is known as #winning... or #punching

It feels very exciting because we try hard to close the gap and get to 7 so that we can stay with them. We become smarter, hotter and more charismatic, as we raise our own bar. When we raise the bar, our self-esteem goes up accordingly. Unfortunately we tend to attribute this raised esteem to the other person.

Great relationships happen when we value our self at 5 and value the other person at 7, while simultaneously, they value themselves at 5 and they value us at 7. If we kept this up then love could last for ever – if, that is, we practiced managing the energy.

In my case this definitely didn't happen. I was yet to learn about the power of the metaphysical world. Self doubt kicked in and I started to wobble. An inner voice said "Shit I'm actually a 3 or 4. Lancelot will soon find out. This is really stressful". I spiraled down the vibratory scale, to become the Damsel.

Meanwhile, at the start of our relationship, Lancelot probably thought I was a 7 and he was a 6 #winning #kinda. I was super independent and competent, which he probably found interesting. Plus, when we met I had the killer outfit on... the one fashioned by the Fairy Godmother.

Later on, after I'd turned into the Damsel, it was time for battle stations. Shield! Breastplate! Visor! He covered all the bases of head, heart and guts, where any needy energy might possibly get through.

Eventually (inside all that metal) things probably started to feel a bit dead inside, because no life force energy could get in either. Lancelot peeped out of the visor and saw shiny, happy people. He was drawn like a moth to the flame... in full battle armour, so looking seriously hot. Now even 8s were looking at him with a glint in their eye, a toss of their hair and an ambiguous smile on their face.

Lancelot looked at me (in his estimation now down from a 7 to a 4) and looked at all the 8s.

It was a "no brainer".

The identity world with its metrics has to give way to some sort of new system where we learn how to manage energy better. It's not something we've valued before. The old world favoured intellectual ability, so most of us were raised to develop the strength of our mind, not the strength of our heart. The old world valued masculine energy, over feminine energy, but in order to create flow, we need both.

We don't have a blueprint to copy. After all, if we go back to the archetypal realm of Camelot, the only three expressions of feminine energy were as follows...

Guinevere

In archetypal terms she's the Child. First she's the good girl (sweet natured, obedient and kind). Then she falls in love with Lancelot and becomes the bad girl (spontaneous, rebellious and selfish). Outcome – she spends the rest of her life in a convent, apologising to God for her lack of impulse control.

The Lady of Shalott

In archetypal terms she's the Damsel. She is imprisoned in a tower and cannot interact directly with life, or suffer death as a consequence. Outcome – she falls in love with Lancelot, activates the curse and dies.

Morgan le Fay

In archetypal terms she's the Sorceress. We'll get to her in the next section. She is the preserver of shamanism, magic and the nature world. She has to fight to keep the patriarchy in balance, but she's also in love with Lancelot. Outcome – she is shunned by her brother the King, rejected by Lancelot and has her whole philosophy of life ridiculed as religion and the rule of law are established.

This Unholy Trinity needs to be transformed if "the future is feminine" and if we are relying on feminine energy to save the world.

These three archetypes, sum up our fear of where the expression of our feminine energy will lead us...

Guilty. (Guinevere)

Trapped. (The Lady of Shalott)

Humiliated. (Morgan le Fay)

We're familiar with the negative aspects of the feminine, and the positive aspects of the masculine, so it's no wonder that both men and women flocked to undertake the Hero's Journey. I was one of them. It *looks* really impressive.

The screen of competition. The mirror of narcissism

But after Lancelot left, I found myself staring at the computer in a different way...

Where is he? What is he doing? Who is he with?

And staring at the mirror in a critical way...
Am I a 5 or a 3? Could I become an 8?

I was trapped behind glass.

Under a spell.

Just like the Lady of Shalott, I thought that if I broke the glass I'd die.

My soul whispered...
Break the glass and you'll find out how powerful you really are.

But I hadn't yet learnt how to hear that voice.

CHAPTER 10

Total eclipse of the heart

We need new words.

If we had new words, things wouldn't get so confusing. There is conditional love and unconditional love. We call them both love, yet they are very different. All love in the physical world is conditional love.

Friendship love

We're friends with people who like us. If someone criticizes us or doesn't like us, that pretty much signals the end of our love for them.

Love of things

We love things that make us feel good. Once they lose their capacity to do this, we discard them for new, better things.

Romantic love

When we fall in love we see ourselves reflected positively in our lover's eyes. This improved, version of ourselves makes us feel high. Once the mirror becomes tarnished and reflects back a diminished version of who we are, we feel low. Just like Snow White's stepmother, when her magic mirror told her she wasn't so lovely anymore, we become angry, sad or sulky, depending on our emotional style.

Sexual love

Lust happens when we're unselfconscious and in a world of our own. Because of this it's often easier to achieve with someone we don't love. When we love someone we care about them so are tuned in to what's going on for them. Not only are we self conscious, we're "other" conscious. This sometimes makes it difficult to get lost in an out of body experience.

Spiritual love

Our love of God is the most conditional of all. We want him to answer our prayers and meet our needs. We get disappointed if he doesn't deliver on the special service agreement that we paid for with our devotion. Some people conflate loyalty to him with suffering for him... leading to a masochistic form of love.

ALL these versions of love are Identity Love. In the physical world, our heart is just a pump, a few inches in diameter, that circulates blood around the body. In the metaphysical world our heart extends into the energy field that surrounds it. We flow energy from our heart into this field, then we experience that expansion as love.

It's easier to grasp when talking about things. If we love a pair of shoes, they make us feel great. If we decide they're not fashionable and throw them to the back of the wardrobe, they don't make us feel anything, because we don't value them any more. If a friend comes by, brings them out and declares they are amazing, we look at them with new eyes (loving eyes!) at which time we fall in love with them again.

THE SHOES HAVE NOT CHANGED! We changed our perception, our appreciation. We changed the energy that we flowed towards the shoes.

We could use this same principle towards people, but we usually block the energy we flow towards them with judgments and expectations. When we fall in love, it's easy to assume that the joy we feel comes from the other person, but joy lives inside us. Lancelot is a bit like a soul chiropractor, aligning and opening the energy channels so we can experience more.

However, once the energy channels open, old repressed needy patterns can emerge. This gives us an opportunity to grow beyond them. We don't rise to this challenge very often, because we find our own neediness too painful.

We're familiar with the concept of "no pain, no gain" but is pain really necessary? Sometimes animals are wiser with their strategies for growth. Take sea crabs. They have a ridiculously hard outer shell. When it's time for them to grow, they squeeze themselves out of this, leaving behind a shell suit of body and legs, and emerging as a "soft shell crab". Obviously this makes them extremely vulnerable to predators, soft shell crab being something of a delicacy.

In order to avoid mass extinction, they do their growth and rebirth process together. Crabs, previously known for their solitary, hermit like existence, gather in their thousands to make a huge crab mountain. The ones on the outside act like Roman gladiators, shielding the ones on the inside as they shed their shells. In this way they guarantee the survival of the species.

Girls have adapted this strategy. When one of their friends has their heart broken they gather around her with ice cream, duvets and Prosecco, speaking hilarious, heartwarming words of encouragement. This is how they survive.

IT'S OK I'VE GOT THE FERRERO ROCHER

Unfortunately I couldn't draw on this support network because I couldn't admit to anybody that I'd been having an affair. When my boss got back from New York, he was different. Every now and then he'd flirt, but he developed an air of extreme busyness. My self esteem plummeted, but I kept lowering the bar on my expectations until I was living on crumbs. I was hyper sensitive to his moods, which would determine if I had a good day or a bad day. Watching him charm clients made me feel jealous, and desperate for his attention.

Falling in love with your boss is a cliché for a reason. We're unschooled in power dynamics and nowhere are power dynamics more evident than in the workplace. We don't see people as they are, we see them as part of a broader context. Our energy doesn't have clearly defined boundaries – that's just an illusion, which is why context plays a big part in attraction. Someone who's a God on the beach, when transposed to an urban setting will appear naïve and unsophisticated. Similarly a guy who's King of the boardroom will be incompetent and awkward on the beach. We're always experiencing the energy in the gap... the energy of the context as well as the person.

Projection is a big part of relationships. My boss was charismatic, but he was also moody (I projected that he was grappling with inner demons)... and selfish (I projected that he was super intelligent, so easily infuriated by the stupidity of others). I realized the way I'd compared my kind boyfriend to a shark like predator and chosen the latter because it made me feel more alive. But the aliveness came from fear, adrenaline and context... not love. We may interpret yearning as love, but we're actually experiencing our needs... and our disappointment that the other person is refusing to meet those needs.

The only way we solve this conundrum is to become better at managing the energy. We hate neediness in ourselves and we hate it in others. This begins in childhood. When a small child cries with fear, anger or disappointment we try to control the energy "Oh look...a teddy bear, an ice cream, a Disney video. Please stop crying, I'm being triggered." When we grow up, we carry on the same pattern. "I feel lonely, inadequate, unattractive... what can I buy, eat, watch, to make me feel better."

Successful relationships happen when we manage the energy in the gap between us. Relationships teach us how to balance and transform this energy. Problems arise when one partner doesn't want balance, they want competence. They don't want to be in a play with different storylines, they want to be the Knight ALL THE TIME.

ASSUMING THE POSITION

Understanding this made me realize how much I'd been stuck in an either/or world, playing the Knight in the relationship with my boyfriend and the Damsel with my boss. I handed in my notice at work. I no longer wanted to be part of the magic dust and the power dynamics. My boss wasn't sad about me leaving, he was merely irritated by the inconvenience it caused him.

My boyfriend was pleased I quit, because he'd been worried about me. I felt ashamed and grateful in equal measure. When I looked in the mirror I did look gaunt and pale, like somebody who'd been vampired, except it wasn't my blood I'd been donating, it was my energy.

I started noticing the amazing qualities in Percival, the qualities I had stopped valuing. Just like the unloved shoes that I'd relegated to the back of the wardrobe, I looked at him with new eyes. Once I did this, I fell back in love with him.

Unfortunately, it was too late. He chose this moment to tell me it was over, and he was leaving. He'd been waiting for the right time and now that I was out of my stressful job, and feeling better, there was no reason for him to stay.

That's when the mirror cracked.

SECTION TWO CONCLUSIONS

Identity

When it comes to falling in love, projection plays a huge part, both in the way we present ourselves and the way we see others.

We yearn for metaphysical things – freedom, spontaneity and creativity – but when we interpret this through the identity world, we fall in love with archetypes that have traditionally encapsulated these qualities... like the pirate, the cowboy and the artist.

Steve Jobs summed this up as "why join the navy when you could be a pirate". We associate being a pirate with someone flamboyant, brave and sexy, whereas actual pirates hijack oil tankers... they're cruel and unattractive with bad teeth.

Projection is a powerful spell. It's important to separate identity and energy if we want to avoid being seduced by a powerful brand.

Choice

The blueprint for the Knight/Damsel pattern is laid down in childhood.

When I fell in love with Lancelot, it triggered the way I felt as a child, waiting for my Dad to come home... curious about life in the outside world, excited, ready for fun, games and adventure– that's the archetypal imprint of the Knight. Beneath that was an older pattern, the way I felt as a baby with my Mum... helpless, vulnerable and dependent – that's the archetypal imprint of the Damsel.

We can't escape these vulnerable feelings inside us, so we repress them. Both positive and negative aspects of masculine energy are deemed acceptable, because they're familiar. We love the positive aspects (focused, driven and decisive) and so we allow the negative ones (rigid, independent and self-serving).

We're less familiar with expressions of feminine energy in the outside world, so we diminish the positive aspects (loving, inclusive and intuitive) and we demonize the negative aspects (passive aggressive, emotional and needy).

Because we all have both masculine and feminine energy, falling in love is a way to bring repressed energy to the surface. When we're welded to an either/or perception, we play Win/Lose. It's a bit like musical chairs... someone gets left holding the needy energy that no-one wants. It's obviously not pretty for the loser who is now drowning in the depths, but it's also not ideal for the winner, who has to rely on willpower to make waves on the surface.

In the metaphysical realm, we could use this as an opportunity to end the win/lose game, keep dancing with the energy, and ultimately allow creative energy to flow into the gap between us.

Story

Our love stories still follow the old Hero's journey, which is based on...

"getting" (to have and to hold onto) "endurance" (in sickness and health) and a clear "finish line" (till death us do part).

Our new love storyline (the Hero/Heroine's journey) would be based on...

"giving" (flowing love to the energy field) "joy" (playing in that field) and "endless creativity" (directing the energy in new ways). The endless creativity is the Holy Spirit, which arrives when the two forces of masculine and feminine energy unite inside us.

Our masculine storyline is rigid. Sadhguru puts it this way "Women enter a relationship hoping the man will change and men enter a relationship hoping the woman will never change". On a physical level, change means a loss of vitality and beauty, but on a metaphysical level, change means constant growth, creativity and spontaneity, which makes life interesting. It's important we don't get these wires crossed.

SECTION THREE

Looking for Freedom in Spirituality

CHAPTER 11

In case of emergency, break glass

It was inevitable I'd end up looking for God. They say there are no atheists in foxholes and I was in a pretty deep one. This is the part of the Camelot story where Guinevere banishes herself to a convent. Unfortunately, I had commitments – a mortgage and debts to pay off. Also, having dismissed my childhood projection of God (the impressive guy Michelangelo painted on the ceiling of the Sistine chapel) I wasn't sure who to pray to. I needed to find my own version of the creator, to ask why he or she had created me to be so damn impulsive.

This is when I really started to understand the lack of precision in the either/or perspective. In the corporate environment, impulsivity was called spontaneity and in a work force of procrastinators, this was valued as a skill, not a flaw. Similarly telling a client we could deliver when we couldn't (and had to make it up on the way) was considered courageous, not what it actually was... a lie. In the metaphysical world, energy doesn't separate into good or bad. It's there, or it's not there.

The same applies to relationships. We try to fit them into the either/or world. In a divorce case, courts decide who is the good person and who is the bad person according to their behavior, but it's their energy that's the most important thing. If one person withdraws their energy, the other person feels abandoned... even though they're in the same room. This is where the phrase "the person who leaves a relationship is the second person to leave" comes from. When my boyfriend left, I had no-one to blame but myself.

By now it was 2001, the year envisioned as "the future" in Stanley Kubrick's film. I needed to work, but I was drowning in the worst kind of emotions... heartbreak, neediness, guilt and regret. Luckily by this time the internet had been invented. There are an awful lot of solutions for mental distress on the Internet, so I'll condense them. Like everything else in the either/or world, they fall into two categories.

In the masculine corner... the Self-development, Motivation guys, spearheaded by Tony Robbins. *Become a master of your own destiny. Take control of your life. Hack your way to a super charged you.* The jargon here is very masculine and contains a lot of exclamation marks – Killing it! Smashing it! Nailing it! This space is dominated by The Mind.

In the feminine corner... the Self-love, Heal your life women... spearheaded by Louise Hay. *Rescue your inner child. Attract abundance. Magnetize your soul mate.* The jargon here is very feminine (although they copy the exclamation marks) – Love! Feel! Surrender! This space is dominated by The Heart.

What kind of choice is this?

In 2006 a small book called *The Secret* became a best seller. It proposed an end to the Hero's journey of striving, suffering and endurance... just "Ask, believe and receive", because "thoughts create reality". Metaphysics entered the mainstream. Everyone got excited about having the power to create wealth, heal illness and attract the perfect partner.

Like so many so called "new" spiritual ideas, this one is mentioned in the bible *"And all things, whatsoever ye shall ask in prayer, believing, ye shall receive"*. However, now it resurfaced with some fancy new branding, so it was taken seriously. *The Secret* sold over 30 million copies. People loved the idea that they were magical beings, capable of creating their own reality.

It didn't work... obviously. There's a difference between actually being able to create magic and being fascinated by it. It's easy to see where the fascination began...

1   We stopped believing in a gender specific God who had an identity (a big man) who lived in an actual place (heaven) and who punished evil. Obviously this was ridiculous – far from being punished by God, bad people were getting away with murder.

We became disenchanted... which led us to search for enchantment.

2   The rapid growth of technology made us feel robotic and programmed... like hamsters on a wheel, constantly scrolling, while the news reel kept turning. The power of The Man was increasing. Despite the labour saving promises of technology, most people were working harder than ever.

We yearned for a super power, to unhook us from this trap.

3   We became disappointed in the traditional health system. Despite technological advances, people weren't getting any better. Alternative energy practices started to thrive. Once people believed in acupuncture and herbal medicine, it was just a hop, skip and jump to the more magical processes of chakra re-aligning and aura cleansing.

We longed for a fairy godmother to cure our ills... not pills.

4   Things were going badly wrong with the environment. Climate change and crazy weather. Pollution of water, earth and air from plastics and chemicals. Animals, birds and fish struggled to survive. They were dying in droves because of human greed and we were powerless to stop it.

No wonder we wanted a magic wand.

Religion and Magic have been in competition over the energy world for a very long time.

Religion has always been ruled by masculine power. Women couldn't be trusted. They "had the devil in them," and had to be controlled for their own good. Before the Summer of Love, their only access to power was to marry it. Girls were raised to be obedient, passive and slightly masochistic.

When Guinevere married Arthur, she was set for life. Everyone wanted to be Guinevere. "Blonde, beautiful and married to the King" were the popular three wishes, should a genie show up with a magic lamp. Talking Barbie dolls of the sixties were programmed to say the aspirational words *"Let's plan our dream wedding!"*

Another positive aspect of the Summer of Love was the emergence of a completely different archetype – Morgan le Fay, the sorcerer. In the preceding years, the patriarchy had portrayed witches as bad, ugly and frightening. They wanted to make "the force" as unattractive as possible to women. With the resurrection of Morgan le Fay, they became sexy, powerful and appealing.

Blame it on my teenage years reading Lord of the Rings; blame it on my twenties when I was in love with Led Zeppelin and Fleetwood Mac, but the world of magic, elves and faeries has always pulled on my heartstrings. It was natural that I'd be drawn to new age spirituality. It looked so much like the enchanted realm. There were high priestesses talking about astrology and Avalon, crystals to keep away negative energy or attract good vibes and rituals around the phases of the moon!

All traditional religions have rituals where energy and identity collide with interesting results. The Catholics have...

Confession. Enter a small dark confined place, tell an anonymous person all your bad thoughts and deeds and come out feeling a whole lot better. Energy cleanse, in return for a few "Our Fathers."

Communion. (Follows confession – after you empty out the bad stuff, you can fill the void with good stuff.) Eat a wafer, which has literally been transformed from flour and water into the body of Christ. Feel the union and bliss of oneness with God.

Baptism. Wash away sins with water. Instant soul transformation and lifetime guarantee of access to Heaven.

Pilgrimage. Follow a well trodden dusty path. Endure blisters, sleeping on hard ground and inadequate food supply. Receive enlightenment.

Though the literal interpretation leaves something to be desired, energetically, these are all based on sound principles. Having rituals adds focus if we want to let go of guilt (bad energy) and connect to love (good energy).

The New Age brought in their own version of these rituals… based on the same principles, but with more branding, marketing and money.

Psychotherapy. Enter a room with certificates on the wall. Tell an anonymous person all your bad thoughts and deeds. Feel better, for a short time. Pay a lot of money. Buy a package as it's cheaper than individual sessions and you've been told it's going to take a very long time before you're properly healed.

Workshops. Enter a room with lots of people. Judge everyone instantly. Own back all your projections. Feel the union and bliss of oneness with God. Pay a lot of money. Leave the room, at which point all the projections come back. (They were just waiting outside the door, like naughty children.) Sign up for another workshop.

Rebirthing. Lie down in a labour ward of shouting, crying people. Hyperventilate until you almost pass out from too much oxygen. Feel slightly ridiculous and pretend to have a spiritual experience, so as to not be left out. Feel a failure and a fraud. Re-book because you might just get it next time.

Pilgrimage. Follow a well trodden path on a comfy tour bus with regular pit stops for organic food and ethnic jewelry shopping. Pay a lot of money. Feel wonderful. Go home to live with Muggles. Feel bored again.

I'm not saying there's no value in any of these, but we need some discernment... particularly if we have a shopping addiction.

If the old religions featured a controlled, obedient child, the new ones featured a very self indulgent one. It seemed we all wanted the Harry Potter version of spiritual power, not the one with all the discipline.

We want to do the magic tricks, without the hard work.

Ridiculous in reality, but totally available on the internet. (Webinars to Find Your Inner Magician available on You tube, everything else available on Amazon.)

Just click.

Like Dorothy (Ruby slippers available on Ebay.)

This marriage of technology and spirituality has made everything a whole lot worse.

CHAPTER 12

Must be the season of the witch

I approached the healing of my heart in the same way I'd approach a project at work (like a Hero). In other words, research the options, find the best product, work out the quickest route and set off on the journey. Because technology has advanced faster than our biological capacity to keep up with it, it's difficult for us to control our impulse for instant gratification... and instant healing.

We could have done with a visit by a Ziggy Stardust alien to download us with some new software around the turn of the century. Instead, we got Harry Potter. This just increased our desire for magic, while reinforcing our frustration of life as a Muggle.

WHAT WE NEEDED   WHAT WE GOT

Around the same time that people began talking about *The Secret*, scientists started talking about the gut microbiome. They discovered that the trillions of bacteria in our digestive tract determined everything from our mood to our immune system. Intelligence was no longer restricted to the mind and heart, there was now a third centre of intelligence. Because of this, the term "gut brain" was coined.

The mind brain is good with knowledge, the heart brain has emotional intelligence and the gut brain has instinct or "inner knowing". We kind of already knew that our mind wasn't the only intelligent thing about us, which is why we say "I knew in my heart it wasn't right" or "I had a gut feeling this would turn out well". We refer to "mother's intuition" or "gamblers gut". These terms come from the Energy world. Now they are being verified by science.

As we took up residence in our heads, we disconnected from our gut brain. This was a huge mistake. Our minds might be clever, but they don't know how to make our fingernails grow, or our kidneys work, or even how to get our lungs to breathe in and out. All these things happen while we're asleep and our mind is off duty.

The gut contains our connection to life force energy. Everything in nature is fuelled by the same life force energy. It's really intelligent. We only have to look at a David Attenborough documentary to realize quite how intelligent. Creatures with tiny brains are capable of extraordinary feats. They know how to fly in formation, travel to destinations they've never been to before, correctly identify poisonous plants, create geometrically perfect webs... they can even predict changes in the weather.

This is because they're connected to an intelligence that is beyond their small brains. The reason we humans find it hard to access this intelligence is our need to be in control of our own little domain. We love our independence, so we disconnected from the life force.

There's a reason that Shamans, Wizards and Witches have a close connection to nature – whether that's the animal kingdom (familiars) the plant kingdom (herbs) or the elements (earth, wind, fire, water). They understand and respect that, though our minds are clever, there is a far superior intelligence connecting every living thing.

The religions of the world also knew about this intelligence, but they turned it into an identity (God), and they came up with all sorts of stories about what "he" wanted. Things like...

1 He didn't want us to have creative power (no eating from the tree of knowledge).

2 He didn't want us to have sex or money (Sex is sinful and money is the root of all evil).

3 He wanted us to be obedient and follow "his" rules.

It's easy to see how this male God was a projection of the type of guy The Man liked to hang out with. Someone who knew a thing or two about keeping everyone in line.

If our energy channels were more open, the gut brain could provide access to genius level creativity. This usually only happens when something dramatic or complex occurs. If our mind brain is overloaded with complexity, and the heart brain is paralyzed with emotion, sometimes intuition can blast its way through.

There are numerous examples of this. Those who've experienced it describe it as being "taken over" by something else or "entering a flow state". There's less of their individual identity and more life force energy. Perhaps this is how Captain Sully managed to land a plane on the river, after both engines failed, saving the lives of 155 passengers – an incident dubbed "the Miracle on the Hudson". He went metaphysical, allowing him to make lightening speed calculations that were proven to be better than those of the most sophisticated computer.

In the physical realm, miracle is the closest word we have to describe this kind of phenomenon.

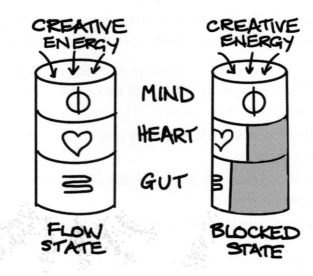

The gut brain is extremely complex. Physically, there's a whole eco system of intelligent life going on down there that scientists are only just beginning to understand. It isn't just a load of tubes that process food, it's a highly complex system containing trillions of cells, neuro-transmitters and intelligence. It sends more messages to the mind brain than vice versa. Currently it's on autopilot for survival, but if we connect our gut brain to our mind brain, and make it more conscious, we could access the power to create miracles.

The mind rose to prominence at the beginning of the 18th Century in *The Age of Enlightenment*. During this time, the intellect ruled. It was a logical extension of King Arthur's vision. Magic, mystery and the supernatural (Morgan le Fay's vision) were outlawed. If you couldn't see it, hear it, taste it or touch it, it didn't exist.

For example, in 1847 Dr Semmelweis recommended that doctors wash their hands because he suspected that germs (invisible things) were killing his patients. This was considered to be so ludicrous that he was committed to a lunatic asylum, where he died after being beaten by the guards.

Many of our so called "enlightened" ancestors had a complete disregard for any intelligence that wasn't human (e.g. micro organisms, animals and plants). They even considered women and indigenous tribes to be less than human. This allowed them to objectify and rape the planet with impunity.

The indigenous tribes, watched this take over bid in confusion. Their decisions were made for future generations. They thought that drinking your fill and then poisoning the water hole was a crazy strategy. Even if a few young bucks thought this would be fun, they were educated by the tribal elders.

We have no tribal elders, because no-one wants to be old any more. We want to be young for ever. We're all about our identity – something The Man exploits to maximum capacity (The anti ageing business is currently a $200 billion industry).

We need our gut wisdom now more than ever, but the gut also holds our greatest fears and unconscious desires. We're making some progress with revealing the inside of our hearts... these days we can be honest about our emotions of loss, heartbreak and even jealousy. But we've made very little progress with the gut, because the feelings trapped down there are worse – humiliation, revenge and rage. We're less inclined to own up to them because that would REALLY mess with our identity.

♡ Feeling upset because someone has hurt you is acceptable.
⧤ Wanting to make someone else suffer is not.

♡ Feeling insecure or lacking in confidence, is acceptable.
⧤ Humiliating yourself in a really embarrassing way is not.

♡ Feeling a bit lonely and disconnected is acceptable.

☰ Destructive or self destructive death wishes are not.

We avoid our dark impulses and favour the light. We avoid the moon and favour the sun. Witches have always been associated with the moon, offering honour and respect as they fly past on their broomsticks. Shamans have always preferred the company of the moon for rituals. They say the veil between the visible world and the invisible one is thinner during the night time.

We were not raised to respect nature, as a powerful life force, which has infinite capacity for creation and destruction. We were not raised to understand the balance of masculine and feminine energy within us, just the different roles and identities of masculine and feminine gender.

We were never introduced to the Goddess Kali, the destroyer. Our only female deities were gentle, meek and mild... long suffering mothers who endured, maidens who were obedient, elders who were ignored.

Because Arthur triumphed over his sister, we were taught to fear the power of the witch.

It's time for her to return.

CHAPTER 13

Witchy woman, see how high she flies

How did this patriarchal stitch up happen? That would be a whole other book, so here are some of the highlights.

In 1590, King James VI was sailing back to Scotland, after a trip to Norway. There was a terrible storm. Because James was a nasty piece of work (think Joffrey from Game of Thrones – over indulged, cowardly and terribly cruel to vulnerable people) he decided that the storm had been caused by women in league with the devil, who wanted him dead.

This theme of women being in league with the devil is as old as Adam and Eve, but King James caused this to jump to a whole new level of crazy. To cut a long story short, he had 100 women arrested and subjected to the most horrific torture possible.

The "witches bridle" was invented. The logic was that the bridle worked to tame wild horses, so it would do the same for wild women. This bridle consisted of metal straps that went around the face and a metal bar containing four spikes that was forced into the mouth. Two spikes went straight into the tongue and one spike pierced the side of each cheek.

Being metal, the bridles could be fixed to the side of the prison cell, ensuring the wearer had to stand up and was unable to sleep for days and nights (not that you'd be able to drop off if you could sit down – this was just for added cruelty.)

Eventually, they confessed to whatever King James wanted them to confess to.

Yes I met the Devil in the church at night. Did I concoct a spell from a cat's scrotum? Absolutely. Sex with faeries? Why not. Just get the spikes out of my face and stop tearing my fingernails out.

Once he had their confessions he had them burnt at the stake – because according to their confession, they were witches. He had the signatures to prove it. Pieces of paper – physical things – triumphed over energy, so that law and order could be restored.

King James VI, and all his supporters, were probably scared of an energy they didn't have a name for, didn't have an understanding about, and didn't have access to. Their actions therefore would have been driven by fear, ignorance and ultimately jealousy.

It gets worse.

After acting as judge in the witch trials, James went on to endorse witch hunting throughout the land. He wrote *Daemonologie*, the definitive guide. This wasn't a short opinion piece, but a long, serious, theological doctrine about the need to find, and kill any woman engaged in witch-craft. For good measure it also described how to find and kill them.

Evidence for being a witch was tenuous to say the least. A mole on the skin was proof of a love bite from the devil. Easing the pain of childbirth with herbal tea – definite sorcery (because the Bible says that God wants women to suffer.) Cooking a casserole over an open fire (bound to contain eye of newt and toe of frog.)

If there was any doubt about whether a woman was a witch or not, the book advised binding her hands and feet and dunking her in the river. If the accused didn't sink or drown, she was definitely a witch (because holy water repels evil so would not accept her into its watery depths). The confirmed witch would then be untied and burnt at the stake.

Of course the flaw in this plan was that if they were "innocent", they drowned, so they died anyway. In the 50 years that followed 3-4,000 so called witches were killed in Scotland alone.

The most shocking part of this story is that the malicious, misogynist that was King James VI went on to edit the Bible, and his version – the King James Bible – is the one that is widely distributed and preached from today.

You couldn't make this up. When women look at their mild mannered ancestors and say "Feminism… what took you so long?" this is possibly one of the reasons why.

When feminism arrived (in the Summer of Love) women reclaimed their sexuality. The invention of the birth control pill, allowed them to enjoy sex without the fear of pregnancy. It also freed up a lot of energy… when women (in the western world) stopped having ten children, they could direct their creative energy into other things.

If control and structure represent the identity world, then sexuality fits more easily into the energy one – out of control and complex. Women are more biologically connected to the energy world, because they have to receive the impulse to push during childbirth. In pagan times, they were assisted in this labour by midwives (later called witches, as men rushed to assert their authority over the female reproductive system).

The easiest way for the church to control women's sexuality, and their connection to the energy world, was to create two contrasting identities – the Madonna and the Whore. If you weren't in the former category, you were probably in the latter, and could be treated as an undesirable low life. Motherhood was the only gig in town. This caused a lot of problems which we're still trying to iron out.

Going back to Camelot for a moment. When Arthur became King, there was equality for a while between Pagans and Christians. Arthur and his Knights brought rules, law and order to the marauding tribes that threatened to invade Camelot. This was a good thing, but their success made them think that this was the ONLY way to manage "out of control" energy.

THE BOOK OF MORE MEN

As Arthur and his knights became more rigid and determined to solve every problem with laws or cold steel, Morgan le Fay, the sorcerer, was relegated to the outside of the golden circle. She wasn't exactly bridled, but she was silenced by being demonized. In the male version of the story, she became jealous, angry and bitter. But then again, this was often the way older women were portrayed in stories written by men. Older women must be jealous of the maiden's youth and beauty, because youth and beauty are things highly prized by older men.

Morgan le Fay and the Celtic Goddesses were resurrected and legitimised in the Summer of Love. But this is just another identity. We've flipped the archetype of the Witch from bad to good. We separate things into either/or because we can't get our head around the fact that we live in an energy world, and energy doesn't have borders.

We cling to the identity world, where children are innocent and good (in reality they can be manipulative and aggressive); where the hero is selfless and courageous (in reality often narcissistic and self serving);

where nature is butterflies and flowers (again, mosquitos, poison ivy, earthquakes).

We all (both men and women) have the potential for violence, vengeance and cruelty inside us. It's good that we've become civilized, but most of us haven't transcended our destructive side, we've just repressed it, with unfortunate consequences. Repressed energy can turn against us. Anyone who has suffered from self hatred, self attack or depression knows how destructive this energy is. Anyone who struggles with addiction knows where it leads.

Repressed energy causes blockages in our energy system. This limits our creativity and the righteous rage, that would allow us to change the world in creative ways. We get angry about things, but then the anger quickly peters out. We're scared of the dark side of energy.

It was a good idea to resist the patriarchy, reject the masculine interpretation of the Bible and re-instate the Goddess. It was a good idea to realize that we can access the power to heal ourselves, heal others and heal our world.

It was a bad idea to be seduced by the identity of magic. Real magic (miracles) requires us to transform old survival patterns in our gut brain, so we can become a clear channel for the energy. It was a bad idea to believe that higher consciousness could be achieved through self indulgence, crystals, magic wands and workshops.

Of course, back then I didn't know any of this, so digging out my floatiest dress (Stevie Nicks circa 1980) I signed up for my first workshop.

CHAPTER 14

Workshop Woe

For the spiritual seeker, there are many types of workshop, and I tried a lot of them. This has less to do with the fact that I'm thorough in my research, and more to do with the fact that I'm a highly addictive person. At least workshops were a healthy addiction, not like cocaine or co-dependent relationships.

Joining the new age community was a bit like starting in the music business, and then the corporate world... slightly bewildering at first, because there's a lot of new jargon to learn. After decades in the harsh masculine worlds of music and marketing it was lovely to be welcomed into the tribe of "the divine feminine".

Although workshops differ, their themes are the same – the need to heal pain, ditch limiting beliefs and become empowered. This makes sense as most of us have been hurt, feel inadequate and wish we were more successful. Early upbringing is always a feature, as this is where patterns start. Few of us were given sufficient praise as children, the kind of praise that would have stopped us forming the belief that we're not good enough.

I'm not sure where I am on this debate because some of this is down to context. In the past, many parents had a hard enough time making sure their kids stayed alive. These days, parents go to the other extreme, and are over the top with their praise, which brings a different set of problems. Their children can grow up to have absurdly high expectations of others and very little resilience to criticism.

I put this thought aside because it is always the loveliest thing in the world to be on the receiving end of praise, and people in workshops are lavish with their compliments. They tell you you're wise and wonderful, magnificent and extraordinary. These are all good words to say to your soul. Unfortunately, if we are not connected to our soul, the words are received by our identity. It's no wonder our identity loves the journey of healing. So much so, that it probably doesn't want to end the journey and actually be healed... not yet anyway.

Healing involves getting to the root of physical or emotional pain, by discovering our childhood patterns. We are attracted to the qualities of the person whose love we craved the most. In my case, Lancelot represented my Dad who was elusive, always working or doing things that didn't include me. Some part of me believed that if I could get Lancelot to notice and value me, I'd complete this unfinished story with a happy ending.

We withdraw from people who display qualities that remind us of love that made us feel bad or guilty. In my case the Lady of Shalott represented my Mum, trapped in a house knitting cardigans for small children. I shrank from needy people... I was shrinking from myself now that I had become one.

As well as a love pattern, we also have a fear pattern. If we were bullied as a child, we either fought back, or we befriended the bully. We learnt to face our fears with aggression or compliance. This means that later on, as adults, we stay in unfulfilling jobs, because they give us status (the status of being Top Dog) or because we're scared to leave (thereby becoming Lap Dog).

This revelation (often occurring during a workshop) caused quite a few people to realize they were in the wrong career and needed a new, more fulfilling one... moreover, they didn't want a career, they wanted a "life purpose".

Many of these people looked at Tony Robbins (who has been producing epiphanies like rabbits out of hats for some time) and decided they wanted to be just like him. Unfortunately only Tony Robbins can be Tony Robbins, so copying him is just more identity creation. This didn't stop thousands of people leaving their jobs and setting themselves up as healers and spiritual gurus. With supply exceeding demand, healing became very competitive.

I ignored this red flag, as I was so carried away with the good vibes. Huddles over cups of tea and biscuits, warm smiles, and love everywhere. At the end of my first workshop I was walking on air, having successfully let go of all expectations, judgments, anger and sadness. It was just like being high, but without the drugs and the hangover.

I lied about the hangover.

Two days after leaving the workshop I was frustrated, disappointed and angry all over again. I missed Percival, and I hated myself... how could I have been so stupid as to fall for Lancelot? I was nothing more than a ridiculous cliché. Of course this meant I needed another workshop. Apparently my heart had opened, (hence the lovely feelings) but now it had closed again.

No-one spoke about the gut, where the roots of my negative feelings were busy throwing up new shoots like it was springtime on steroids.

I developed a new pattern... go to workshops, open my heart, lose all my sadness, anger and guilt, feel love for everyone who'd ever hurt me, rejected me or withheld their approval, go home, feel terrible again. Rinse and repeat.

I was a child, not a sorcerer. Instead of getting in touch with what was going on in my gut, I did this yo yo dance between my head and my heart. Instead of going deeper into myself, I went further in my research, because there were always better, more exclusive workshops. Some were set in special locations, where the very stones are portals to higher realms. Inca burial grounds, Tibetan monasteries, Indian ashrams. It all gets a bit expensive, but by then I was addicted to the vibes, the travel and the shopping... crystals, singing bowls, ancient relics. All infused with juju, magic and healing properties.

Meanwhile my in box was groaning from a tidal wave of marketing as each new influx of spiritual teachers searched for customers. There was a lot of identity around the archetype of the Sorcerer. The female version had renamed itself High Priestess or Goddess. The male version stuck to Wizard, as it had none of the ugly connotations of Witch.

By now, having experienced a lot of workshops, I realized where the real magic was. When people come together, lose their identity and become more open hearted, they experience bonding... true connection, which is powerful. But this would happen regardless of the workshop topic. They could come together to make tomato soup and the magic would work.

Whenever I spoke to attendees about their best workshop memories, they always spoke about the participants they met, the lifelong friendships they'd forged, rather than the content of the workshop. Attributing the feeling of bonding to a Guru or his/her methodology is the opposite of empowerment because it's giving power away.

This is why I became disenchanted with it. Or maybe I just have an aversion to marketing. Marketing and God have always made strange bedfellows.

I'm ok with false promises when they relate to chocolate bars or face cream. "Yes, it will give you energy!" "Yes, it will make you look younger!" But the chocolate bar costs very little money, and if you are ridiculous enough to believe that a moisturiser has the power to turn back time, then more fool you. Even Cher can't do that, and she's pretty awesome.

Spiritual principles work, but they involve work...

If "thought creates form", and 95% of our thoughts are unconscious ones, this is a problem. Our mind may be creating miracles but when our gut is creating mayhem, that's a lot of mayhem. Becoming more conscious of what's going on in our gut brain would be a good place to start.

If "we're all one... all part of the same energy" that means we should respect, protect and love the planet, because a symbiotic relationship with it, is essential for our survival. The pagans, druids and sorcerers may not have been intellectuals, but at least they understood that. Being an eco warrior on social media without changing our buying habits or our behaviour, doesn't help.

If "what you forgive in others, you forgive in yourself" (because we're all connected) then forgiveness sets us free. Unfortunately, when we're not in touch with our gut brain, we only forgive with our head and part of our heart, which means our capacity for forgiveness is very limited (mostly reserved for people who take our parking space... Namaste, asshole)

Jesus said "You are Gods". This means that, like God, we have the power to heal and to create. Perhaps if he'd said "you have the potential to become Gods" or "You are Gods... in training", things wouldn't have got so out of hand.

Words again. The new testament of the Bible has about 138,000 words. Jesus said about 24,000 of them. I'd like to say the difference between these two numbers is the stuff of legend. But it's actually just the stuff of patriarchy, and that really good friend of the patriarchy... marketing.

CHAPTER 15

The gut ... it's all about sex and money

In the identity world we place a high value on sex and money. If something looks sexy, it's more desirable. If something is expensive, it's more valuable. When these principles are transferred to spirituality, we get charismatic leaders, exclusive healing programs and expensive workshops. Not because they're good, but because if they were cheap, or readily available, nobody would believe they were any good.

This idea of "Because you're worth it" is fine, when the marketing is aimed at wealthy people, but not so fine when the marketing is generic and sweeps up a lot of vulnerable, poor people in its wake.

Our propensity for projection is ok when we're projecting onto a rock star, because the cost of admission to a concert isn't too high and you get a lot for your money - a serious lighting rig, fabulous sound and pyrotechnics. But when we project glamour onto Leaders or Influencers, the "value for money" becomes questionable. It's ironic how many self-help gurus, who teach workshops on abundance, received their wealth from selling workshops on "How to be abundant".

There are no end of influencers who promote magical spiritual life-styles, all beautifully photographed in exotic locations, with fabulous accessories.

You could of course just sit and watch your thoughts... like Jesus did for 40 days in the desert. Or you could disconnect your phone for a few hours. These are both great ways to become more aware of the gut brain, which will start screaming its resistance in a matter of minutes. Neither of these options is very glamorous, which is why people spend $10,000 to go to what is laughingly called The Oneness University (reach God through your wallet).

In the physical world, if you have sex appeal or financial wealth you can climb the ladder to a lifestyle of the rich and famous. You can finally declare your freedom, because you aren't answerable to anyone. Obviously you won't *feel* free because the only part of you that can feel free is your spirit... and that's still trapped inside someone you don't like.

In the metaphysical world, power is all about the ability to change reality through focused intention and creativity. You don't seek gold, you become the goose that can lay golden eggs whenever they're required. Doing this requires an open mind, an expanded heart and a more conscious gut.

Our only problem is lack of courage. When I think of courage, I picture people doing brave physical acts like climbing mountains or fighting dragons. These images have become familiar. What takes real courage these days is to sit and watch our chaotic thoughts; sit and feel our negative feelings; sit and fight the urge to raid the refrigerator. In other words, clear our three energy centres, so we can be a channel for creativity. I'd sign up for a mountain climbing holiday in a heart beat, but sitting for an hour a day is excruciating for me. I'm bored, irritated and my mind obsesses about a hundred things I could be doing instead.

Because of this, we project our yearning for the metaphysical onto the outside world. We fall in love with creative people, or we buy things creative people have designed. We follow healers, or we buy programs that healers have devised. We bring creativity and healing down to the physical realm through the IDENTITY of creativity and healing. We add the word *creative* to a job title on a business card. We add the word *magical* to a website profile. "I don't just do business coaching, I'm a business alchemist!" People are no longer computer programmers they're Ninjas, no longer consultants but Gurus and Wizards.

This is all identity. We refuse to go inside, where we could transform our gut brain from survival mode to creative mode. At the base level, our survival instincts are expressed in the urge to mate, and the fight for territory (or sex and money). This strategy has resulted in over-population and war.

The way old world religions dealt with sexual energy was through repression. This had disastrous results from child molesting priests to the proliferation of porn. The way old world religions dealt with money was also through repression. Because it was "the root of all evil" it was advisable to go without or give it to the church.

The way new age spirituality dealt with sexual energy was to elevate it, to LOVE. Climb the ladder to the higher frequencies, and take the sex with you. The term "sacred sexuality" was born. Unfortunately we live most of the time in lower frequencies. This is why the Summer of Love failed. In the bliss of a drug high, we transcend our animal nature. Everything is energy, "oneness" and sharing. Once the drugs wear off, and we come back to the physical world, the idea of sharing our boyfriend is a crazy concept. We become jealous and possessive.

The way new age spirituality dealt with money was to elevate it to the realm of ENERGY. "Money is just energy... allow it to come and go" rolls easily off the tongue of the Guru, until his promoter steals some of that energy, then it's very much about the green stuff after all.

The energy of survival is both creative and destructive. We create (money/babies), and we destroy whatever threatens them. The strategy of The Man is to *control* the energy of creation and destruction. Sex is good for creating more consumers. Making money keeps capitalism alive. Destructive energy can be directed against opposing forces.

If we collaborate, and connect to the higher frequencies of love, we can use our destructive energy to bring down corrupt systems and our creative energy to imagine new ones.

Spiritual workshops can be wonderful, in the way rock and roll concerts are wonderful, not because of the Guru, but because of the energy. When people have a common focus or intention and forget their private agendas, love arrives in the gap between them.

Single agenda... legal high

Jesus said *"when two or more are gathered together in my name, there I am"*. He meant the LOVE would be there. Old world religions interpret this as the ACTUAL Jesus (SO literal)... despite the fact that they all seem to agree that God is love.

Two people, (or lots of people) with a single, focused intention can rise to the higher frequencies of creativity, love and healing.

It doesn't work if we PRETEND to focus on the same thing, while secretly harbouring private agendas. Then it seems as if the love has gone, but in reality, we just left the place where it was.

Different agendas – chaos and fighting

It's easy to feel high on love in a church or workshop, because everyone's focusing on the same thing. It's more important to excavate what's going on down below... otherwise we'll always be at the mercy of its gravitational pull.

Jesus was a master of the metaphysical realm, so he could transcend the either/or laws of physical reality, where everything has a fixed identity – matter or energy, particles or waves. He could transform energy to matter and matter to energy, thus walking on water or healing the sick. He had the power to create and change reality.

He also spent a lot of time in prayer and meditation, which is kind of a pre-requisite for performing miracles... it takes commitment to transform our "kill or be killed" survival patterns.

Generous prayers, like "May everyone find peace and happiness" (as opposed to needy prayers like "Please bring me money and a boyfriend") have the energy of love, which always raises our vibration. Meditation (having no thoughts) basically restores us back to the factory settings of our divine nature, before we became trapped in the lower frequencies of survival, scarcity and fear.

Prayer and meditation require discipline, which is why we prefer the Harry Potter version. We want special magic wands (Holly with unicorn hair core) special jargon (Expelliarmus!) and special workshops (Hogwarts).

To emulate the mystics (the true alchemists), I decided to sit and be with myself. I went inside, past my experience of being hurt, and I fell into something much worse... an awareness of everything that I had done to hurt other people.

I remembered all the events that I'd reframed, in order to show myself in a more favourable light; the times I could have responded with love, but chose to withhold it; times I knew somebody else wanted validation or kindness but I chose to turn away and make myself busy; times I lied to save my skin and make me look more competent than I was... and at the bottom of this hell was betrayal.

A famous Italian poet called Dante depicted the journey to the underworld as 9 circles of hell. If we're going to explore the gut brain, it's a good place to start. On his descent down the spiral, Dante met liars, frauds, thieves and murderers, people who had been greedy, lustful and violent. But the very deepest part of hell was reserved for betrayers. That's how much God hated them. That's how much I hated myself.

It was a difficult pill to swallow.

The shame was almost too much to live with. The new age spiritual tribe were no match for its dark power. And so we parted company. I think they were happy to see me go. I was too rebellious, way too opinionated, and I could spot a fake Morgan le Fay at 20 paces.

After all, I was one myself.

SECTION THREE CONCLUSIONS

Identity

The need to turn life force energy into an identity is hard wired in us. Representations of God are an old paradigm attempt to build a bridge between the metaphysical and the physical, because of our child like need for God to have a face, and for that face to be masculine.

If we see God as a powerful person, who can help us or ignore us, we can become needy or angry. If we see God in ourselves, we can become spiritual narcissists. We want to demonstrate our healing and creative abilities, not because we love our fellow human beings, but because these skills make us look very impressive. Also it means we can adopt a fancy spiritual title, channel off planet beings and be all Namaste on social media.

Deep down, we believe the story that we're bad people who made God angry when we ate the apple from the tree of knowledge. We feel guilty and ashamed for no good reason. On top of this self-hatred we paste a fabulous identity.

If we do something that doesn't match our identity (something that tarnishes our "brand") we hide it in our guts, whether that's binge eating, attraction to porn, self pity, rage or vengeful fantasies. This trapped energy sends out low frequency vibrations, without our conscious awareness, thus creating a lot of mayhem in our outer world.

Choice

If the either/or of love is Independence or Dependence, the either/or of spirituality is Good or Bad.

Either we are born bad (in original sin no less!) and must become good, or we are born good and gradually become bad. Our tools to transform from bad to good, are the carrot and the stick. We are praised or punished into transformation. Unfortunately if we're praised, we don't believe we deserve the praise so we dismiss it. If we're punished, we just develop a really bad attitude.

As far as religion is concerned, sex is also in the good/bad category – good if you're married, bad if you're not. But sex, being energy, doesn't respond to rules. The energy is there, or it's not there. This means the reverse might be true – no energy if you're married, lots of energy when it's incredibly inappropriate. This is a bit of a conundrum for the physical world, but a great opportunity for the metaphysical one, as it allows us to practice managing energy... summoning it when it's not there, and directing it in creative (rather than destructive) ways when it is.

Energy is neutral, but just like electricity, if it's not being directed consciously, it can also be destructive.

Story

We are energy beings having a temporary experience in a physical body. As such, we are all on a journey back to God, but the journey isn't linear. Jacob's ladder was a metaphor. The serpent didn't seduce us into the fall from grace. God doesn't actually play snakes and ladders. The story in which we are bad, guilty and unloveable, and therefore must suffer for our sins, has to go. Similarly the reverse story... the one in which we are special and magical, and therefore entitled to have all our needs met by the outside world. That one has to go as well.

Our new story, is that we are consciousness expanding into infinite possibility. We have the capacity to be co-creators of this evolutionary process, or victims of it. We can connect to the creativity of high frequency energy, or we can connect to the pattern repeat of survival thinking. If we're creative, the outcome of our choices is unknown, but if we're in survival mode, we will never feel fully alive.

We realize our potential for expansion by making our energy stronger than the pulls from the outside world. Distractions and drama draw our focus in all directions, leaving us with insufficient energy to direct our own lives. We have to call our energy back from the places we've invested it... e.g. the unfinished storylines of past relationships; the anxiety of earning enough money, or the hypnotic trance of 24/7 social media coverage.

The physical world is visible and fixed. It seems to have a lot of power, but this is an illusion. Banks, Corporations and Religions could easily collapse if we stopped believing in them. The metaphysical world is ephemeral and fluid. It seems to have no power, but this is an illusion. It is a grid of highly creative energy, capable of processing an infinite number of permutations.

If we practice, we can decide where to focus our energy, rather than let this be determined by the outside world. We start by shining a light on the hidden, fear based agendas of the gut. With a balanced mind, a loving heart, and a gut that's connected to life force energy we could create a whole new story for humanity.

SECTION FOUR
Call off the Search

CHAPTER 16
Identity 3.0 ⏀ Real You

Fifty years have now passed since the Summer of Love, when the statement "I want to find myself" first became popular. It's over 400 years since William Shakespeare wrote "to thine own self be true". Clearly the concept of "Being yourself" has been with us for some time.

"Being" is a metaphysical principle, because it's about energy, and energy just knows how to be. The problem with humans is that we're energy inside a physical body, with a creative neocortex that is endlessly trying to find, prove and imagine things. Trees and animals have no problem being themselves. Dogs don't feel inadequate because they're not horses. Apple trees don't beat themselves up for not producing pears. Angst about being better, or being true to ourselves, is a human thing.

Our body and mind aren't "who we are", they're a vehicle for consciousness. Who we are is the energy driving this vehicle.

Confused energy being in an identity world

As we grow up, we create an identity by developing the parts of us that gain the most attention. We imagine ourselves as the protagonist in the story we are living. Then we become our identity... and forget who we really are.

This is like Meryl Streep watching herself in the Devil wears Prada, and saying "God I hate fashion. I wish I could be Meryl Streep", while we all scream "But you ARE Meryl Streep!"

Our mind is like a film director, constantly assessing our performance, criticizing and giving us endless notes on how to play our part better.

We squish our energy into an identity in order to operate in the physical world, but we never feel as if this identity fully represents who we are... because it doesn't. We have many selves inside us. Some of mine are quite contrary. If I'm in a room full of fearful people, I pull out the maverick, whereas super positive people bring out the cynic. "To thine own self be true" is a bit of a conundrum for me. I'm not so much looking to "find myself" I'm more "meet the team".

Recently a lot of social media space has been taken up with the need to "Believe in yourself", but again who are you believing in? You (your energy) or You (your identity). Social media is all about identity. We curate our life to show the good bits, the highlights, the exciting trailer to the less interesting movie.

And how about "being true to yourself". By what criteria? The "responsible, hard-working" self – is it really responsible or just scared it might be irresponsible?... is it naturally hard working or just needy for approval? Is it a truthful expression of energy or an acting out to prove an identity?

Our identity is often a reaction to who we DON'T want to be. I became a Knight because I hated the Damsel. If I had befriended her, loved her and allowed her to become part of Camelot, she wouldn't have become unhinged and self destructive. Energy we judge, reject or abandon usually goes rogue and comes back to bite us.

We need an identity, to create as an individual, but we should make this identity as fluid as possible, so that life force energy can come through and animate the full expression of who we are. Unfortunately this clashes with the standard, current advice, which is to "become as nice as possible or no-one will like you" and "become as niche as possible or no-one will find you". Neither of these are conducive to becoming more real, they're just conducive to becoming an impressive brand. Which as we know from a previous chapter is a made up thing – the opposite of real.

The time before selfies

We have two modes of thinking – logic and creativity (sometimes referred to as the masculine and feminine sides of the brain). Our logical brain is a data bank. It's associated with the past because it contains things we've memorized from school or discovered through personal experience. Our creative brain is our imagination. It's associated with the future because it allows access to infinite possibilities... the unknown.

Most of our identity is constructed by the logical side. We figure out what our skills are and build an identity on top of them. Logical analysis is valuable, but our creative side has an equal vote in our thinking.

Unfortunately, most of us weren't taught to develop our creative side, so our powers of imagination default to a negative setting. We project past mistakes onto the future, and we imagine worst case scenarios.

To make matters worse our gut brain (being sensory) can't tell the difference between real events and imagined ones, so it reacts like we're in a war zone, flooding our body with stress hormones 24/7. Stress hormones, like cortisol, shut down the neocortex, further hijacking our attempts to be creative.

Who was the real me? Rock chick, damsel, shaman, pioneer, bitch, badass, strategist, faery queen, sinner, saint. All of this and more. What should I do now? I checked my phone constantly, for evidence of which version of me would bring the validation I craved, but it no longer brought relief.

The screen of a smart phone encourages the warped logic of comparing how other people LOOK (glamorous and impressive... IDENTITY) to how we FEEL (unhappy and anxious... ENERGY). Of course we can't compare how they feel, with how we look, because that's not how the screen and mirror work.

Snow White's stepmother had a magic mirror. This mirror told the truth – revealing the inside of Snow White (pure and good) with the inside of the stepmother (wicked and cruel). In the Disney version, the mirror compared their identities... Snow White young and beautiful, the stepmother past her prime, and clearly in need of expensive age defying beauty products. Disney and The Man are close bedfellows, because merchandising is just so lucrative.

When we break our addiction to the screen and mirror, we become less reliant on approval from the outside world. This allows a more real expression of "who we are" to emerge.

CHAPTER 17

Choice 3.0 ♡ Real Love

Technology has allowed us endless choice, but what's the value in this if we can't manage the energy of choice and end up with decision paralysis? If we have to make all decisions from the either/or level of consciousness, our mind and heart will want different things. If we suppress the heart, there's no desire, so life feels boring. If we suppress the mind, there's no plan, so life feels anxious.

Every choice creates a "what if" scenario, which drives us crazy. If we procrastinate and see saw between mind and heart, our gut will choose for us. The default setting of the gut brain is habit and survival. It won't choose wisely, creatively or courageously, it will choose whatever feels familiar or safe.

It's amazing how much energy we waste in this scenario. Our heart wants to be happy. Our mind is like the parent who offers ice cream after we've eaten all the broccoli. It says *"You can be happy after you've made enough money and turned yourself into a much better version of who you are now"*. Our gut knows that no amount of money or self improvement will be enough to satisfy an aggressive mind with a big stick in his hand. So the gut says *"Fuck it, let's go straight for the ice cream and self loathing, we're going to end up there anyway"*.

Our immature hearts need to expand. If we want to feel love and happiness, heart expanding exercises like *Forgive. Let go. Be grateful* are a good idea. Forgiveness frees us from carrying the heavy burden of resentment. Letting go provides a vacuum, so that new things can come in. Gratitude fills our energy field with love, which means the new things we magnetise will be lovely things, because like attracts like. The mind may be aggressive, but it's logical, so it has no problem with any of these.

The heart on the other hand seriously struggles with them. If someone hurts us, we want to punish them. Emotion is energy in motion. We don't want to be the one left holding the hot potato, we want to throw it back. Forgiveness and gratitude seem impossible. Letting go feels like losing. It's easy for the mind to say "Let Go", it isn't the one experiencing a painful emotion. The mind may say "accept and move on" but the heart says "rage and cling".

Still, I was determined to practice what I'd learnt in all those workshops, and be all "love and light" about having been dumped by Percival, so I arranged to go to a gig he was working on. He came down from a lighting rig to say hello. In that moment, he was manly and competent... totally in his element. I thought of my boss, who in this situation, would have been out of his depth and vulnerable... desperate to return to the safe haven of his pixelated world and his adoring clients.

My heart lurched. All acceptance of my situation was batted away to be replaced by hope and the possibility of a reconciliation. That's when he pointed to his new girlfriend, who gazed at him from the side of the stage. All my commitment to "love and light" went out of the window, followed quickly by the "gratitude", leaving just chaos and fuckery in their wake.

Self help books often stress the importance of making decisions from the heart. Joseph Campbell advised everyone to follow their bliss, but this advice is firmly rooted in the either/or realm. Joseph was a bit short on information about how to earn money while wandering around in a field of butterflies. And what if your bliss led you to a passionate tryst in a stationery cupboard? The heart can make as many stupid decisions as the head.

As I stood in front of my (now ex) boyfriend and his new girlfriend, I tried to be open hearted and just feel whatever feelings came up... there was surprise, regret, loss, sadness and jealousy. I stayed in my heart for about seven seconds, then I flipped into my head and went into fake mode. I dazzled everyone with my funny, benevolent identity. Then I went home with my hot potato of energy and opened a bottle of wine to go with it.

Needs are painful. Either we rise above them through denial and positive thinking (shifting from heart to head), or we numb them out with our addiction of choice (descending from heart to gut). Denial and positive thinking is fake mastery... under this, we still feel enslaved by our needs. Real mastery comes from "being with" the needs without projecting them onto others or without acting them out... having a tantrum or running away. Real masters hold negative emotions, literally love the hell out of them and transform them into light. That's why they glow.

These days, we're quick to relieve our inner neediness with the dopamine hits provided by technology. We jump every time the phone pings, hoping for a message that will make us smile and feel loved or appreciated... despite the fact that 95% of the time the phone is pinging with boring or unwanted stuff. This inability to hold tension in our body, turns us into slaves.

The moment between the ping and the disappointment is the joy of possibility... a brief glimpse into the both/and world... the intensity of fully inhabiting the "now" moment, before the moment turns into the fixed reality of someone selling PPI insurance.

We could practice living in the energy of possibility, without the need for external things to relieve us of our uncertainty. We could learn to live in the flow of life instead of creating energy from adrenaline and dopamine. Both these strategies require us to give up control of our small world and trust in the bigger game of the both/and realm, where we are both Slave AND Master. When we embrace this paradox, we become the Master of our own energy and Slave to the energy that drives all life...

Slave to the Rhythm.

There's a strong argument, that if we don't achieve this aim, we'll just end up...

Slave to the Algorithm.

This does not end well...

CHAPTER 18

Story 3.0 ⊜ Real power

We need a more up to date story for the times we're living in. Our old story was the battle between good and evil. Perhaps our new story is the battle between between real power and fake power.

In a weird way, technology often feels more real than life. Nature documentaries are more interesting than nature... mainly because we're getting the intensity of the highlights. Lions spend a lot of their time just being, but we prefer to watch the sex and violence, not the "being" part.

If we visit a foreign country, we feel as if we already "know" it because we've seen it as a backdrop to countless movies. This stops us fully experiencing it. We project images from our data bank of thoughts, a split second before we are about to experience them in real time. Meanwhile, we're losing our ability to be present in the "now" moment.

In this age of increasing technology, we are becoming less inclined to tackle the messy business of engaging with humanity face to face. We hide behind screens, becoming less skilled at managing our emotions as we become more seduced by the things we can control. But if we want an intense experience of life, we have to expand our capacity to contain and express both creative and destructive energy.

My habitual response to difficult emotions was to disconnect from them. If I couldn't leave physically, I'd leave energetically. I ran away from boredom, irritation and difficult conversations. At one end of the scale the boredom became mild depression. At the other end of the scale the irritation became mild anger. As soon as I hit either of these markers I'd be off... before going anywhere near something as powerful as rage.

MAJOR   MILD   MILD
DEPRESSION DEPRESSION BOREDOM IRRITATION ANGER RAGE

Perhaps female rage is different from male rage because the female of the species has to protect her young. She has to have enough rage for herself and her cubs. That's a lot of rage. No wonder so many women close off their capacity to feel it. But repressed rage can flip into depression. When we're disconnected from this aspect of the life force, we become "loose cannons" capable of the destruction of others, but mostly, capable of the destruction of ourselves.

There's far more suicide than homicide.

We have a conflict of interest. We want to feel connected to our source, which is creative life force energy, but we're seduced by the counterfeit version... connection to the live stream of a smart phone. Our phones provide safe connection. They feed us dopamine hits of praise and contain our rage by condensing it into emojis.

This isn't satisfying on any deep level, which is why we feel empty and hungry for something we can't describe. We try to satisfy this hunger with things that we can buy or things we can eat. But our spirit doesn't want more, it wants EVERYTHING, because it knows itself to be part of everything, part of the life force.

If we interpret energy needs through a physical lens, we can never have enough. We always want more.

This old story of disconnection from energy, and consumption of physical things, will inevitably have to end because...

1 It doesn't satisfy our craving for deep, meaningful experiences. *These require connection.*

2 We are no longer able to keep a lid on all the rage, which is currently exploding through the weakest links in humanity. *Disconnection is dangerous.*

3 The world will run out of resources, given our capacity for *endless consumption.*

Our new story requires us to develop the inner resources necessary to master our energy... Self Esteem (for the mind) Self love (for the heart) and Self respect (for the gut).

⏀ **Self esteem** means we have to start valuing our creative expression. At school we sang *Amazing Grace.* Grace was so amazing that it "saved a wretch like me". A wretch is an unfortunate, despicable or contemptible person... after colluding with this fact, it's no wonder so many of us struggle with self esteem issues.

♡ **Self love** is even more tricky, because until we expand our hearts, our definition of love is trade. Love is good when the trade is equal and painful when it's unequal or unrequited. Therefore self love is a kind of vague nonsense... I mean how can you trade with yourself? That's why most people's version of self love is just self indulgence.

Self respect is trickier still, as this requires self forgiveness for all the things that made us lose respect for ourselves in the first place.

In our old story, the hero leaves, competes to prove he's better and wins the prize.

In our new story, heroes will come together to form communities of shared interest. They will use their rage to fight a common enemy

(The Man) and use their creativity collaboratively, thus sharing all the prizes... love, abundance and lots of energy.

When we watch children playing, it's easy to see how they share the same collective noun as baby goats (kids). They have so much energy, they can barely contain it... running, colliding with each other, jumping over things. As kids we hate going to bed (*Just five more minutes! Please!*) As adults we hate getting out of bed *(Just five more minutes! Please!)* What happens to us when we grow up? (Answer... we disconnected from the life force).

In the physical world, if we give someone a slice of our pizza, we have less pizza. In the metaphysical world, if we give someone energy, we create more energy. Kids know this. If we smile, other people smile. If we start laughing on a train, everyone starts laughing. On the other hand if we walk into the office angry and sulky, pretty soon everyone is unhappy. Energy is expansive. Used wisely, it can change the world.

As I sat on my yoga mat one morning, I realised what I wanted to do. I would help people discover the story they were currently living in and support them to create one that better represented the whole of who they would become...

A true love story, with glory and fuck ups, jokes and Jesus. A mystical story, with a guiding star, more than three wise women and a winged David Bowie singing *We can be heroes*. A never ending story, in which the spells of the Man are broken, fear and need are diminished, and depression is liberated. I knew my way around in the dark.

I would become a road manager of the Underworld.

CHAPTER 19

Camelot revisited

If the three brains had archetypal counterparts in the Camelot story...

The mind brain would be Guinevere and Arthur – two aspects of the Child archetype.

The heart brain would be Lancelot and the Lady of Shalott – two aspects of the Lover archetype.

The gut brain would be Morgan le Fay and Merlin – two aspects of the Sorcerer archetype.

The task for the Child is to grow up and face the fact that all choices have consequences, but we have to choose anyway. The responsible child has to let go of the need to control. This is scary, because outcomes are unpredictable. The irresponsible child has to conquer trigger-happy impulses for bright, shiny objects or bright, shiny people. This is difficult because... marketing. We're worth it (because we're great) and we deserve it (because we're unhappy.)

The Lovers have to manage the tension in the polarities of independence and dependence; desire and letting go. When emotion arises, one will cling while the other will run away, but it's the same emotion they're both dealing with. Lancelot needs the courage to take off his armour and show up with his energy. The Lady of Shalott needs the courage to step away from the mirror, and rescue herself. This is difficult because marketing has convinced us that love means excitement, lust and yearning.

The Sorcerer has to form a better relationship with power. This means becoming more honest about hidden agendas in order to become a clearer channel for true creativity (not creativity that is self serving and makes us look magical and impressive, but creativity that acts on behalf of the whole). This is difficult because marketing has sold us the "identity" version of power. Marketing also panders to our habits, compulsions and addictions, which keep us from the discipline required to access high voltage creativity.

Marketing just causes SO many problems. It's no wonder we find it hard to get aligned. Luckily Camelot has also provided a couple of sacred objects...

One Feminine (the Holy Grail).
One Masculine (the Sword Excalibur).

In the Camelot stories, the knights searched high and low for the Holy Grail but could never find it because they were asking the wrong question. One of the knights (Percival) discovers its location in a concealed castle, guarded by a wounded king. He is called the Fisher King because he is wounded in the groin and can no longer do any-

THE GRAIL

thing but sit by the water (like Narcissus) and fish. The king is impotent, his land is barren and he is waiting for magic to heal him.

Metaphorically, the Holy Grail is the energy of the empowered feminine, which has been missing from the world since Christianity, with its trio of Masculine Gods took over. The Fisher King represents the wounded masculine – dysfunctional sexuality, and disconnection from the creative life force. The church repressed sexuality and creativity, so this blockade of unprocessed energy, could have created the Fisher King's wound.

Being stuck in a repetitive pattern that lacks passion and inspiration is the kiss of death to the part of us that longs to feel alive. When we see the human spirit in action, we're *moved*, because this is *love in action...* Firemen running into burning buildings. Shy people delivering a TED talk. Students taking on The Man over the insanity of gun laws, pollution and global warming. These things make us want to cast off our fears and do brave, creative, inspiring things. We know, deep down, that we want to live a life that serves others. Love is an active, not a passive, force.

The question Percival had to ask was not "Where is the Grail?" but "Who does the Grail serve?" Or in the words of Bob Dylan *You're gonna have to serve somebody.*

If we don't serve consciously, we will serve unconsciously – we'll serve the power in others (wasting our time and energy following celebrity stories on twitter) we'll serve youth and beauty (wasting our time and energy trying to turn back the clock) and we'll serve the Man (wasting our time and energy earning money to pay for our endless consumption).

We can't not serve. But we do get to choose who we serve.

Next, the sword of truth, with which we should probably kill the Man. Obviously not literally and not actual men – but the old paradigm. Excalibur was a sword of truth, a sword to unite a divided Kingdom, and ultimately a sword to champion the disenfranchised.

Arthur might have freed Excalibur, but the rise of a rigid, rule based world meant that pretty soon, everything else became set in stone.

If the Grail helps us heal our wounded masculine, through acts of service, the Sword empowers the wounded feminine. The feminine has centuries of fear patterns to overcome... Fear of ridicule, abandonment and poverty; fear of speaking out; fear of being burnt alive. These are in our collective DNA. The feminine also has centuries of either/or beliefs to dismantle... that we can't be collaborative *and* successful; we can't be kind *and* powerful; we can't be logical *and* creative.

Fear and doubt create self fulfilling prophecies. For example, people who are given an incorrect diagnosis of a disease, can go on to develop it. But on the other hand, people who are given a placebo sugar pill can heal a disease. The fearful mind can create illness and the optimistic mind can create health.

Perhaps the sword Excalibur was not a magic sword after all, but believing it was magic, made Arthur invincible, because it gave him both courage and confidence. The same is true of ourselves. With practice and a virtual magic sword, we could overcome our fears and change our limiting beliefs.

Acts of service (The Grail) and sacred activism (The Sword) are the way forward. And remembering how important it is to ask the right questions.

Questions for the mind. *Why am I doing this? Really? What will it give me? What will it allow me to avoid?*

And the big question for the heart. *How can I love without expectation?* Because expectation creates need... and neediness just makes you want to fall on the sword yourself.

Lastly, Camelot. In a way, Camelot is its own archetype. It symbolised a utopia of unity, harmony and love. It didn't work out long term, because they couldn't figure out how to deal with the energy of rage. Also, of course, because the Christians turned the philosophy of Jesus "love thy neighbour" into a corporate mission statement, with a very suspect marketing plan, and a strategy of endless crusades and killing.

On the death of her husband, Jackie Kennedy said "Don't let it be forgot, that once there was a spot, for one brief shining moment that was known as Camelot."

It seems that John and Jackie Kennedy made a similar mistake. They loved the identity of Camelot – parties, pageantry and pillbox hats. And above that the grand vision, nobility of purpose and emotive speeches. The reality of course was somewhat different and there were all sorts of shenanigans going on behind closed doors.

Identity looks great. But only the energy is real.

CHAPTER 20
Energy – the future

Pretty soon we'll all come to understand that life works in a different way than we previously thought. We'll realise that it's not just words or actions that determine the outcome of our life, it's the energy behind our words and actions. We'll stop looking outside for inspiration, love and power, we'll work from the inside out and become better generators of inspiration, love and power.

The world will change in ways we can't currently imagine. Some tribes call this "The Awakening", an event foretold by their ancestors. Some religions call it "The Apocalypse". Either way, it's safe to assume that it won't be "business as usual".

There's a lot written about the need for more feminine energy to change the world, but this is often interpreted literally – as the need for more women in governments, corporations and churches. The identity world is interested in balancing quotas (data) rather than balancing energy, so many women who rise to positions of power do so using masculine energy.

Masculine energy (when it's positive) is focused and forward moving; rational and logical; it fosters good leadership.

Feminine energy (when it's positive) is creative and nurturing; inclusive and empathic; it fosters vision.

Masculine energy (when it's negative) is aggressive and rigid; independent and self-serving; hierarchical and superior.

Feminine energy (when it's negative) is manipulative and passive aggressive; emotional and irrational; needy and dependent.

It's not a matter of gender or taking sides, it's about uniting both energies inside ourselves and aiming towards their higher frequencies. It's also important to be aware of unresolved, hidden agendas, because all frequencies, whether surface or secret, create an outcome.

In the identity world, leaders of corporations are often referred to as White Knights. Their resumes may be in perfect order, but energetically they can be sociopaths. The words on their mission statements may say "we value people" but in reality their employees are often pawns in their power plays... kept safe only when they're valuable to the game.

Similarly employees of corporations can hide their Damsel behavior behind the words of H.R. legislation. They may cling to jobs they have no real talent for or take unnecessary sick days.

Narcissism creeps into the Corporate World

Religions are still firmly entrenched in the identity world. Arguing about the textbook rules of different religions is pointless, now that we know the level of consciousness through which God's words were first interpreted. All religions share the same principles in the energy world – forgiveness, love, gratitude, generosity. It's only the words that differ... God's name is Yahweh, Jehovah, God, Jesus, Allah, Shiva, Vishnu, Brahma... and this matters (?!) because words are important in the identity world.

We abolished slavery because the idea that someone has the right to "own" another person is crazy and out of date. We adopted feminism because the idea that "women don't have minds" is crazy and out of date. Why can't we do something about religion? It's more crazy and out of date than anything. It is also the source of both these ideas.

When we refuse to sort out our relationship to energy, we'll constantly be seduced by the identity world. In the same way that powerless people voted for the Mafia, angry people voted for Donald Trump. They couldn't process their own rage so they wanted to be associated with his identity of kick-ass bravado.

Child-like thinking...

145

If a government official or a CEO takes a risk and shareholders get rich, he's a hero, if it goes badly he's a villain. Leaders are often paid to make these kinds of decisions, which is why so many of them have "thick skinned" on their CV rather than actual talent. This is an absurd criteria to evaluate people by.

In religious circles, a lot of people are praying for the welfare of the world. God is represented as a powerful but capricious Godfather to whom we petition. "Please help my friend and give me favour." Energetically, the frequency of these prayers is often *need* and *fear*. The universe works on frequency, not words. What we focus on expands, therefore our focus should be on love and creativity rather than need and fear.

An effective prayer therefore, isn't a litany of words. It's a feeling made up of gratitude and love, fuelled by imagination and motivation. It's about resisting the gravitational pull of need and fear, while holding a vision of the future that becomes magnetic enough to draw other people towards it.

Real power (life force energy) doesn't demand that we beg, trade or hate ourselves. It doesn't take sides, it has no sides. It merely says "Come home to who you are. You have been lost in a story of power-lessness, not realising you have all the creativity you need to write a much better one."

This is what the empowered feminine will look like when it arrives. In our history, we've witnessed the energies of positive masculine, negative masculine and negative feminine. It's time for the final, missing piece of the jigsaw – positive feminine. This alone will heal the unconscious story about who we are (*God is good and I am bad*) which is the origin of our unconscious compulsion to hate ourselves.

Unless we form a better relationship to need and fear, we'll never get there, we'll just remain on the surface, distracted and seduced by the identity world.

The things we *think* we need are... money, status, success, popularity, attention and praise. The things we fear are the opposite... poverty, failure, invisibility, rejection, loneliness and humiliation.

Most of what we fear comes from the incorrect or lazy use of our imagination, which imagines these worst case scenarios, but fear can be reframed with creativity and diminished with courage.

It starts with balancing our energy...

The Child and the adult – so we can be spontaneous AND responsible.

The Knight and the Damsel – so we can love at a higher level.

The light and dark Sorcerer – so we can create more wisely.

Balance was a word I used to associate with boredom or sitting on the fence. I preferred the drama at the edges, which is where I looked for freedom. Balance in the energy world requires us to become flexible and fearless so we can let go of control and fully enter the flow of life.

We are energetic beings and our energy has a frequency. The frequency we emanate has an effect on us, on the people around us and on the planet we share. Knowing this, it would be a good idea (for our own health and that of the planet) to rise above fear and practice transmitting the frequency of love... which is exactly what Jesus taught 2,000 years ago.

Much as we'd like to get there with a revamp of our personal brand, there are no short cuts to the contentment he emanated, which is I suppose why they called him the Prince of Peace.

In biblical imagery, peace is represented by a dove, meek and cooing, carrying an olive twig in its beak. But what if it's actually a firebird, singing, as it allows our old identities to burn, carrying the gift of transformation in its wings... the possibility of rebirth into a higher manifestation of who we are.

And what if the alchemy required to release this firebird, is the perfect balance of dynamic feminine energy, supported by true masculine energy, because both these energies are inside us... just underneath the energies of the disempowered feminine and the wounded masculine.

Perhaps this was the message of the crucifixion. Gender is part of the identity world, not the energy world. If the energy could speak, perhaps it would have said...

She is risen.

SECTION FOUR CONCLUSIONS

In the old version of the Hero's Journey, one of the biggest challenges for the Hero, was to avoid getting lost in the unfamiliar terrain. For this reason, he usually carried a compass.

In the "energy" version of the Hero's Journey, our biggest challenge is to avoid becoming lost in thought. We're lost most of the time. We don't generate thoughts, we're at the mercy of whatever wants to pop into our head.

These unconscious thoughts create feelings, which are usually negative – self doubt, irritation, disappointment, boredom. Negative feelings send a message to the gut brain to stay in "safe" mode, which means we can go about the day on automatic pilot.

When we're on automatic pilot, our heart feels abandoned. We "leave" energetically and the survival program in the gut takes over... *conserve energy, don't be creative, be suspicious of everything and everyone.* We no longer feel fully alive. We're in effect sleepwalking through life.

When we're disconnected from creative life force energy, we're easily seduced by the drama of the outside world. We become spectators of life, absorbed in what will happen next... to her, to him, to anyone or anything, as long as it doesn't involve ourselves. We're no longer the Hero of our own story. We live on little hits of adrenaline, but we're well and truly lost.

Fortunately, we have an energetic compass – our heart. When we place our awareness on our heart, and expand its capacity for love, we can shift everything. If we make the heart "mission control" instead of the mind, we can generate new circuits of energy that go from heart to mind and heart to gut.

If we practice feeling positive emotions, the higher frequency of these emotions is received by the mind, which starts generating happier thoughts, and received by the gut, which allows upgraded software to override the old survival program. Mind, heart and gut are now connected and radiating one coherent frequency.

It's a bit like a magic trick – or a magic mirror. We act like a happy, loving, creative person, therefore we look for things to be curious, grateful and appreciative about, therefore the world reflects back evidence of these things. The more we do this, the more energy rises and possibilities increase.

Eventually this state of being can become our default setting. Old survival software is replaced by upgraded creative software. Our vicious circle (life sucks, so the only reasonable response to it is disappointment) becomes a virtuous one (life is a blank canvas I can create onto).

We're no longer lost in thought. Our inner Sorcerer has woken up. Now the journey of life can become far more interesting.

EYE OF THE NEEDLE

Rising to a higher vibration. Heart to mind. Heart to gut.
Gut to higher mind. Repeat. Repeat. Repeat.

PART TWO

——

How to Live in a World Made of Energy

CHAPTER 21

Walking the wire to freedom

If freedom is not a destination, but an energy to be managed, it's important to practice being in the flow of it.

I resisted the concept of practice for years. I was a "seeker" – always living in my head, figuring things out. I believed that solutions to all problems lay in cleverness, determination and having the right map.

"Going with the flow" doesn't mean floating along in a gentle breeze like a directionless hippie. It means going with the energy in all its guises – both the drama of storms and the deadness of the doldrums. Too much energy; not enough energy; and everything in between.

FOCUS

BALANCE

We can't "learn" about energy, we can only practice holding it in our body, until it feels more familiar, and we trust ourselves to handle it.

OVERCOME FEAR

Energy moves along three planes...

Forward and backward.
Left and right.
Up and down.

Going with the flow means being able to make micro movements between these directions and holding the tension between them.

FORWARD
Holding the tension of "not yet"

Going forward, either we procrastinate (because we're not sure what we want and we're bamboozled by choice) or we live in fantasy (we know what we want but it's not coming fast enough).

The energy of "not yet" is a vibration we're not comfortable with. We felt the excitement of anticipation in childhood, but once we became adults with credit cards, there was no need to practice holding the energy of "not yet". We could make most things happen immediately.

I'm fairly ok with taking risks, and holding the feeling of excitement in my body. (In fact it could be said that my love of excitement caused an addiction to romance). It took me a while to realize that it was my love of list making (fantasy) that was stopping me moving forwards.

Before going to bed I would always make a list, which gave me the nice feeling that things were going to be better... tomorrow. When I spent the afternoon in the displacement activity of eating cake, I would make a list of the fabulous healthy regime I was going to start the following day.

Of course I never actually started the healthy regime, I just kept making lists. All my self doubt (why can't I finish this novel?) and self attack (why can't I stop eating cake?) got channeled into the list – itemized, numbered and colour coded. I had no time to sit with my "inner self" and meditate because I was too busy making lists of the amazing things I was going to be doing... very soon.

Eventually (save yourselves years of time) I stopped and sat with my thoughts. It was amazing to discover exactly how much I disliked myself. It was no wonder I spent so much time in fantasy – the future version of me was just so much more likeable than the "today" version. Unfortunately you can miss a lot of your life with this strategy, by simply not being present, where life is actually happening.

Just let yourself be ok, as you are, right now, while being open and excited about the mystery of what's coming.

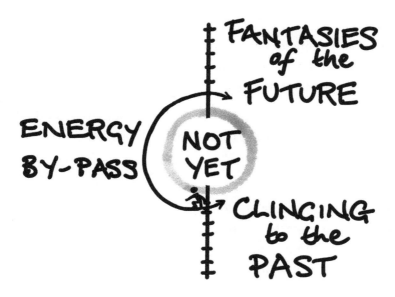

The tension of "not yet".
It can feel stressful or exasperating.

BACKWARD
Completely dropping the tension of "not yet".

Dropping the tension of "not yet" and indulging in thoughts of the past, means there's less stress, but there's also no vision, which makes everything seem pointless.

It's tempting to look back because we can view the past through rose tinted glasses (editing out the bad, leaving in the good) or dark glasses (editing out the good, leaving in the bad). This gives us control over our version of the story. Coming from a Catholic background, I have a large family, which makes this editing process interesting. We were all in the same movie, but we each have a "Director's cut".

We can't edit going forwards, we can only project... usually bad stuff, because our creative muscles are too flabby to imagine all the good things that might happen.

Looking back we can become possessed by guilt (why did I do that?) anger (why did they do that?) or nostalgia (things were so much better before).

Building trust in the present moment, and core strength in our ability to handle the energy of "not yet" takes practice. We would love a magic wand to make the future happen immediately, but these are only available in children's books, and the world needs us to grow up now. (I was going to say Man up but we already tried that with disastrous consequences.)

Try deep breathing and self re-assurance *"Anxiety is just like excitement without the negative self talk. Things are coming when they're coming. Stop trying to control time. Calm down. Let it be. In fact play any Beatles song while you're allowing everything to be EXACTLY AS IT IS".*

Doing this you might notice some really interesting things in the "Not Yet" that you could have easily missed... ideas, curiosities, synchronicities. The mental tension can then be turned into creative tension, which feels a whole lot better.

LEFT AND RIGHT
Holding the tension of "incomplete"

Most of us are trapped in the illusion that something outside ourselves can make us feel complete. Even when our mind knows this is crazy, our heart can't seem to get on board with this truth. We ignore the stories of rich, successful people checking into rehab. We say "I know money, status and relationships don't bring happiness, but they would make *me* happy... because I'm different."

We will always feel "incomplete" because we're part of the universe, having an experience of separation. Instead of trying to end the feeling, it's much better to become familiar with it, because this feeling isn't going anywhere any time soon.

Everything in the energy world is expanding and becoming more of what it is. Interpreting this impulse through the material world means the impulse plays out in the desire for more stuff (to prove we're winning) and at its lowest expression more food (to numb the pain of losing). Neither fills the gap.

Feeling incomplete is an old pattern, so not easy to upgrade. "You complete me" is a standard line in any romantic comedy or Hallmark card. Marriage vows should state "To let go and hold" not "To have and to hold". This makes marriage sound a lot like kite flying, which on reflection, is probably more fun than passive aggression.

Simultaneous letting go and holding on don't make sense in the identity world because they are contradictory things. They can only co-exist in the energy world, once we practice holding the tension of "incomplete".

The vibration of "incomplete" happens in small micro movements left and right... Having. Not having. Having. Not having. It's a balancing act that happens so quickly it seems to be occurring simultaneously.

If we're in a wonderful relationship or an interesting job, it feels great but also scary. We want to lock down the energy into permanent "having". After all the relationship/job might not last, or we might be replaced by someone else. But in order to keep a relationship we have to be willing to let go of it in every single moment.

The obstacles in the way of this balancing act of "having while not having", are the mirror and the screen. These tempt us with the old strategies of win or lose... have and hold on for ever, or lose it all.

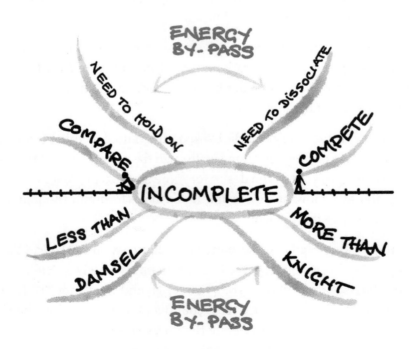

The tension of "incomplete"
It can feel like there's a void that has to be filled.

It took me an embarrassingly long time to get this one because I have a massive ego. If I can't be the best at something, I have to be the worst, and so I became the worst person at letting go. I'm like a dog with a bone. I fight to keep the bone. Sometimes I pretend that I've let it go, but really I just buried the bone, so I can dig it up later and fight with it some more.

This tenaciousness served me well early on in life. Refusing to take "no" for an answer can enable you to achieve extraordinary things. You can cut through bureaucracy like a knife through butter. "Just do it" wasn't something I wore on my sneakers, it was a philosophy of life.

However, when you apply this to people, it's not such a great idea. For years, I refused to let go of the idea that I had lost my one and only soul mate. Really, I am that ridiculous. For the love of God, don't do this. Let go! Now! Nothing will complete you.

It takes practice, but we can inhabit the gap between desire and fulfillment of desire. We can hold the feeling of "incomplete" without going crazy. We do this by micro managing the tension with small movements, slightly left, slightly right. When we do this we can turn emotional tension into creative tension and pour that energy into something else.

We look in the mirror and assess ourselves with kindness. We look at the computer screen and assess the world with kindness. We balance and step forward.

Mirror, screen, manoeuvre.

UP AND DOWN
Holding the tension of gravity and grace

This is the big one as it leads to the ultimate prize, which is freedom. I had tried escaping to freedom, but the thing I was trying to escape from was the energy inside myself so it didn't matter where I went.

I couldn't escape my critical thoughts, my painful emotions and my compulsive behaviour.

Getting high and staying high require discipline. Discipline sounds tedious and boring because we've associated it with obedience (to an external authority figure). But this new kind of discipline is an arrangement we have with our soul, which is loving... being metaphysical, it doesn't have a carrot or a stick.

With discipline we can overcome the compulsion to look down. This allows us to hold the tension between the low vibration energy of habit, and the high vibration energy of grace. We turn survival tension into creative tension.

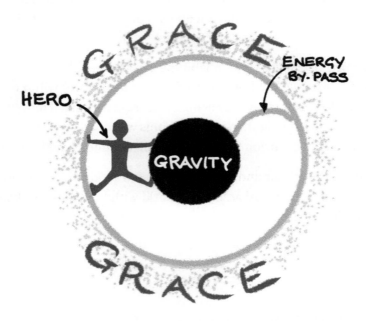

The tension of "gravity and grace"
It feels scary or impossible.

It's easy to feel grace when something wonderful happens, or in the heightened energy of a church, ashram or workshop, but this is often achieved by an energy by-pass, so is short lived. An event pulls us into a higher vibration, but as soon as our circumstances change, we plummet back down again.

Gravity is a law of this dimension. In the same way that apples fall naturally to the ground, left to our own devices we can fall into depression. There is so much chaos in the world, that it's easy to feel despondent, particularly when we place our focus in a downward direction.

On the other hand, things can change very quickly with creativity. Life now is beyond anything we could have imagined 50 years ago, simply because of one invention – the internet. Something invisible, just waiting to be discovered... like all things in the energy world.

Who knows what other amazing things are waiting to be discovered. Life as we know it could change in a heartbeat, so trying to control life with our mind is a crazy concept. We need to become more imaginative, and brave enough to surrender to the creative process that is unfolding anyway.

The energy world requires practice, not knowledge.

50 years ago we took all our knowledge from books, written by the few people (mainly men) who had been taught to read and write. The arrival of the internet changed the game. It magnified everything, which meant more knowledge, increased choice, infinite possibilities and endless consequences. This is overwhelming to our limited intelligence, no matter how smart we are.

Perceiving the world through our mind feels familiar, but it can't help us navigate the complex world we now live in. Even if global problems don't affect us directly, we still feel the effects of them on a subconscious level, because we're all part of the same species.

Life force energy copes well with complexity, so going with the flow is a good idea. This doesn't mean giving up and doing nothing, while waiting for "God" to take over and fix our problems. Allowing human-ity to destroy itself could also be an option. Creators can tinker with a canvas, revise a poem or play around with a melody for some time, but they can also accept it's just not working, and start all over again.

If we become a clear channel, creativity can move through us, without getting stuck. Intuition is received by the mind, it goes through the heart where it picks up the energy of desire, then through the gut where fear has been disabled, and out into the world of form.

This is what is meant by a "Flow" state. Less effort, more ease. Less proving, more allowing. Less endurance, more grace.

Grace is the key word. It isn't the same as the energies we're accus-tomed to (adrenaline and emotion). We can't summon it from where we stand, because it's too high a frequency. We have to meet it halfway.

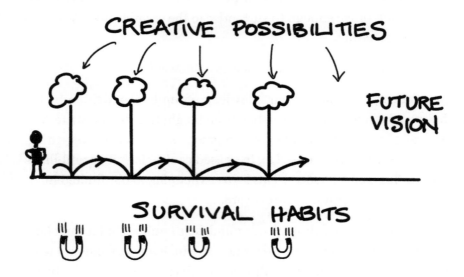

Creative vision. Managing tension. Open to intuition and serendipity each step of the way.

As opposed to...

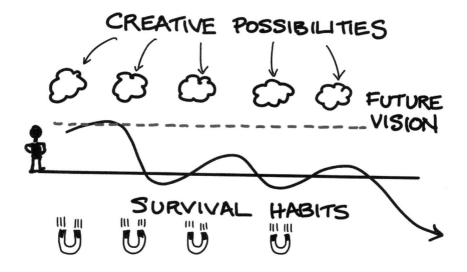

Blinkered vision. Rigid. Ignoring present moment intuition. My way or the highway.

When we're in a flow state we can create more easily because we have better ideas and we're helped by serendipity. If we're connected to life force energy, we're more likely to create things that the world needs (like communities of shared interest), rather than say lighthouses made of sea shells. Please no more lighthouses made of sea shells.

Time to wise up and break some of the old paradigm spells we're under.

"SAD" SPELL BREAKERS

ϕ **Stress (the mind)**

♡ **Anxiety (the heart)**

≋ **Depression (the gut)**

CHAPTER 22

Spell breakers for the mind – freedom from stress ⏀ The Child

No more talking heads

We like to live in our heads, because it gives us the *illusion* of control. The mind is like a child, who thinks with enough focus and concentration, it can keep the plane in the air (oh hang on, I'm still doing that). When bad stuff happens, eg someone else gets the job we want, our mind comes up with a story. Judgment thoughts like *"He's such a dick"* *"I'd have done it better"* or *"It's their loss"* feel empowering, and allow us the illusion that we have some sort of control over the situation.

One of the funny (not funny) things about the mind is that it can only see what it can lose, not what it can gain. If we exercised our imagination, we could respond with curiosity *"Whose thoughts are these? How old am I feeling right now?"* or creativity *"What's the upside? What do I really want?"*

We think we know what we want, but we're actually highly suggestible. Mad men know that if we see an advert enough times, we will come to associate Coca Cola with joy, vitality and having fun, not with the "real" thing that it actually is... obesity and diabetes inducing sugar water, with added chemicals.

These days we're in dangerous territory as we're losing our ability to tell fact from fiction, which is why we need our intuition more than ever. News comes to us in an echo chamber. If we've ever expressed a "like" for something, then the algorithm will keep feeding us the same thing. If we don't develop intuition, The Man will decide both what we buy and what we buy into.

Papa can you hear me?

At some point in our lives, we have all felt childish and disempowered in the presence of authority figures. This is where the expression "Fuck off money" comes from. Work hard and earn enough money that you can tell your authority figures to fuck off. Many of us who spent years on the treadmill came to realize that this was quite a lot of money.

If we haven't addressed our relationship to people with power, our current response is either...

1 To constantly seek approval and validation from the person with the most dominant energy in the room eg bosses or charismatic love interests.

2 To actually become the most dominant person in the room, hence not having to answer to anyone EVER AGAIN.

Sometimes they're the same thing. Donald Trump wants to be the most powerful man in the room, but he's also still a child, trying to impress his Nazi father who thought that bullying was a show of strength and superiority.

166

This leads to the compulsive behaviour of proving ourselves to some real or imaginary authority figure. It also creates a lot of drama and problems, which we can get really busy solving, thus showing how important and indispensible we are.

If we stay in the psychology of the child, we assume that there's a predictable, safe, constant world... if only we make the right choices. This is immature thinking. There is no certainty in the world, so we just have to become more comfortable with uncertainty. If we're scared of making mistakes, desperate for the approval of others, or trying to be right all the time, we'll NEVER experience freedom.

Develop a different relationship with thoughts

We have a voice in our head that never stops talking. Many of our thoughts are negative, because being suspicious, judgmental or critical is our default mode for safety. Most of our thoughts are about the past or future, not about what's actually happening now.

Meditation and mindfulness have become popular topics in books, apps and seminars, but buying and practicing are two different things. Like many people, I tried meditating on numerous occasions but gave up because I thought it was about silencing my mind, which was never going to happen.

However, sitting still for an hour or even half an hour every day and just observing thoughts is a really good option. It gives us an insight into how our minds work. This allows us to realize that though we "have" a mind, we aren't the mind, we're the space in which the mind operates. It's actually quite entertaining to notice the way we think and the thoughts that come and go of their own accord.

The moment just before our next automatic thought is a space of pure potential... with a little practice, we can step into its infinite possibility.

We can become aware of our internal narrator. If we stop from time to time during the day and notice what we're thinking, and how we're thinking, we can make a conscious effort to change the channel to a higher frequency... from critical thoughts to *loving thoughts*.

We can also become aware of our automatic responses when we're in conversation with others. If we pause when someone asks a question (not for a long time as that would be weird) new *creative thoughts* can flow into the gap. We might even surprise ourselves with the answer.

Also, *kind thoughts* are a good idea... it even says so in the bible "Whatever is noble, good and lovely, think about those things". I'm paraphrasing, but I don't trust the King James version anyway, not after what he did to those women in North Berwick.

Make the conscious choice instead of the self-indulgent one

Try detaching from technology for a little while each day. Set the agenda, rather than reacting to the phone's agenda. This sends a message to the gut brain – that our conscious mind is now in charge and knows that validation won't be found in social media or on-line shopping.

We all want to destroy the real villain – The Man – which is virtually impossible given how easy it is to hide if you have a billion dollars in spare change. But one way to hurt him is to stop buying what he's selling.

Ask some better questions. *"What's the real need I'm trying to satisfy? What am I trying to distract myself from?"* Once we look into it, most needs are indirectly about love, self esteem or relief from boredom. There's usually a better way to meet these needs – if we stop being seduced by marketing.

It's time for our inner child to grow up.

It's childish to keep grabbing at the next bright thing or the next new thing. We know deep down, it'll only be new and shiny for a short time, after that we'll want more. It's not the stuff that's the problem (well, maybe it's a problem for the dolphins who are drowning in plastic) it's the hours spent earning money to pay for it... while real life passes by.

Before slamming down the credit card, think of The Man lying on a beach in a tax haven. Do you really want to pay for his next martini?

The easiest way to make a choice is to tune out the distractions and tune in to the energy. Having a quiet mind stops the frantic to and fro. Stops the either/or of indecision. Stops the overwhelm. And eventually...

It stops the stress.

CHAPTER 23

Spell breakers for the heart – freedom from anxiety ♡ The Lover

The Rebel Heart

When our hearts are closed, there's a break in the flow of energy to the gut, which stays in survival mode, blocking our creative output. This means we can have lots of ideas, but we can't birth any of them, which is really frustrating. It also means we stay in control mode, choosing who we love and who we reject. Opening our hearts, allows repressed feelings to surface. Namely...

The intense feelings of neediness when we felt rejected.
The intense feelings of guilt when we did the rejecting.
Underneath these feelings are beliefs, that we're worthless and un-loveable.

It all starts here

It's no wonder that we close our heart and take cover behind a worthy or loveable identity... sometimes being the Knight and sometimes the Damsel.

The Knight shows love by doing things for others... fixing things, giving gifts, selfless gestures... or by fighting for worthy causes. The Knight wears a mask of joy and fun. She likes feedback from the outside world, so focuses on making other people happy. She is loved, but can't feel that love because her heart is closed. If the Knight becomes bitter she can become cynical, rejecting things before they mean too much, rather than risk the pain of losing them.

The Damsel shows love by empathizing, nurturing and taking pain away from others. The Damsel has an active imagination, so can glorify love (putting a loved one on a pedestal and seeing only the good in them) and glorify pain (like those nuns imagining the nails shattering the bones in Jesus's feet). The Damsel longs to feel intense, circuit blowing, ego shattering love. As this isn't available (because her heart is closed) she can fall into self sacrifice and martyrdom.

When we're having a difficult or loveless day we use familiar patterns to manage our anxiety. The Damsel hides, in a tower or under a duvet, seeking solace in junk food and Netflix. The Knight fights unworthiness with self-improvement strategies designed to make her more loveable in the future.

We switch back and forth between the two, hiding ourselves one day, fighting with ourselves the next. If we want to get off the see-saw, we have to uncover our hidden agendas. Ironically, while the mind is a convincing liar, the heart can reveal the truth, which is probably why we keep it closed.

For example, the mind might say "I'm sending this email to Lancelot because I genuinely need to know the answer to this question." When Lancelot doesn't reply and we descend quickly to hell, we know the truth... "I was feeling needy and sent the email so I could experience the dopamine hit ping of a reply".

Break the addiction to the screen and the mirror

This is the place The Man rules supreme. He has employed an army of people with psychology degrees, solely to push the following ideas...

1 Who you are is your identity.

2 This identity is in desperate need of improvement because you're flawed, unhappy and not popular enough.

3 The thing I'm about to sell you is the solution to all of that... it will make you look better or it will relieve your pain.

Who we really are is energy, which doesn't need fixing or rescuing. If we fall under the spell of thinking we are our identity, we become slaves to the screen and mirror.

Stop the comparison and the competition

Just stop. It's not helpful and it's endlessly painful. Nobody else cares about how you look or what you posted, because they're all dealing with their own insecurities.

Do something useful instead... rescue a cat, smile at an old person, throw a party for your needy inner child, dance around the kitchen to 1980s music. Anything. Just throw away the slide rules and the scales. Data won't be impressive in the brave new world – creativity, imagination, and compassion will be. Get a head start.

Step away from the glass. There's nothing to see here.

End the win/lose game

Just as the mind seeks validation, the heart seeks love. Most of us are running on an old pattern...

"If I'm loved, I have value. If I'm not loved, I have no value".

If we make our value dependent on love from other people, we give them power over us. Paradoxically, this means we have to control them, because we've put our self esteem into their hands. It also means we hate them a little bit, because we imagine they've taken our power, when the truth is we just handed it to them on a plate. This is an act of self betrayal which is about as far away from self love as you can get.

Self-betrayal is a horrible feeling. We avoid and repress it by blaming the other person, but repressed energy doesn't go anywhere. If feelings of self-betrayal aren't brought into the light, they can easily turn into self-hatred. Owning an act of self-betrayal is hideous, but not owning it is far worse in the long run.

We may think we're all different and need masses of psychotherapy to solve our very complex problems, but actually we're all the same. People in psychotherapy spend a lot of time and money to eventually be told one of three things *"Your problem is you don't feel good enough... Your problem is you feel inadequate... Your problem is you don't feel loveable"*.

Integrate – when two become one

Love always contains the possibility of loss, because real love isn't about possession... it's a continuous process of receiving and letting go. Sexual chemistry summons life force energy, which moves through us towards the other person. The "loved" feeling comes from being in the middle of the current, not the love object. This understanding takes a huge amount of pressure off both the lover and the loved.

In the sentence "I love you" we associate with being the giver or the receiver of the love. But we could rise above this subject/object duality by being the love that contains both in its embrace... being the verb.

High vibration love is a state of "being in love". In other words, you're not in love WITH anything, you're a Being who is hanging out... in a state of love.

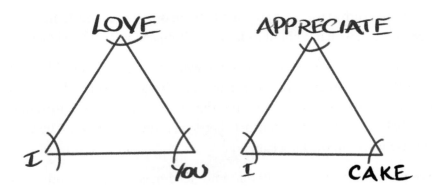

**Be the love. Be the appreciation. Be the verb,
without attachment to subject or object**

This shift in awareness changes our old patterns. Instead of showing love by proving or over compensating, we'll be more present. Instead of making others happy, while feeling depleted, we'll make ourselves happy and share that happiness with others. Instead of rejecting people before they reject us, we'll risk vulnerability.

The Knight will use her fire to fight the ego and its lies of unworthiness. The Damsel will turn her desire into devotion to the life force and become the source of love and creativity. Both will overcome their addiction to the chemicals that their familiar emotions produce... the adrenaline of drama and the dopamine of sentimentality. This is a good idea, because these chemicals are really addictive.

It takes courage to love someone who doesn't need us. Our usual game is to disempower them by becoming indispensible. After all, if our partner doesn't need us, how else do we determine our value?

It also takes courage to love someone without needing them, because it means we have to face our own neediness and work through our insecurities without projecting them onto the relationship.

Noble love seeks the highest potential for the other. It's not for the faint hearted, it's for the sacred hearted.

'Cos the bible told me so

The bible says "To those who have... more will be given". This is a bit of a mind fuck to the literal Christians as it goes against their sense of fairness. But in a way, this is about establishing a new geometry in the body – one where we have an energetic template for the *feeling* of being loveable, the *feeling* of being "enough". Once we change the template of our old beliefs, we can magnetize love, instead of manipulating for it.

This is a far better option than a lifetime spent improving our identity, so that we can "be the best" (lonely Lancelot), or "be chosen" (exhausted Damsel).

We need to experience things, for no good reason; love, for no good reason; care, for no good reason. Not because the images of us doing them will look great on Instagram.

As long as we're human with a human heart, we will always feel needy. Or in the words of REM... *Everybody hurts sometimes.*

Embrace your needs and love the hell out of them... literally love the hell out of them.

You'll find the anxiety just melts away.

CHAPTER 24

Spell breakers for the gut – freedom from depression ➂ The Sorcerer

Define the problem

Depression comes from disconnection from our life force energy. When we're depressed, we feel no joy, and we have no energy, so we swing between effort and exhaustion. Everything feels meaningless. We certainly don't feel free.

Humans are a strange species, because we are animals, but with an upgraded brain which allows us to have individual creativity. This often leads to the worst of both worlds...

1 We are afraid to create because we fear consequences so we don't make full use of our upgraded brain.

2 We have disconnected from our animal brain, which would at least allow us to be content with who we are.

We normally solve this conundrum by working on our mind. We read books on motivation and creative thinking. These haven't had great success because our gut brain has more power than the mind. It doesn't like change, it prefers automatic pilot. If we want to live a creative life, it's more effective to tame our gut brain than plead with our intellect.

Connect to life force energy – the practical stuff

We're designed to be in a homeostatic relationship with life force energy, just like every other living creature on the planet, but we use our creative mind to override this. Our deeper instincts know what to eat, when to sleep and how to move... but we're not listening.

Food. We eat more junk food than real food. There is substantial proof that the ingredients in processed foods cause everything from brain fog to full blown depression. This is a problem because over 80% of supermarket space is devoted to processed foods. We are designed to eat food that comes from nature not food that's assembled in a factory.

The Man makes a fortune from the sale of artificial food, and the drugs required to treat its side effects. The primary function of artificial food is to create addiction. This is allowed because... capitalism. If it has a shelf life instead of a real life, or the list of ingredients is so long it needs a font size you can't read without a magnifying glass, we probably shouldn't eat it.

The gut brain will scream its resistance, but who or what is doing the screaming? Bacteria! The microbiome in our gut contains hundreds of trillions of bacteria, who we feed every time we eat. Left to their own devices these bacteria would create balance (similar to any other ecosystem) because they're connected to the overall governing intelligence of the life force.

We've disconnected from this intelligence because we have an upgraded brain that allows us to make our own individual choices.

We choose food we've become addicted to, rather than food our body needs. This messes up our gut ecology causing good bacteria to die and bad bacteria to proliferate. Now there's even more of them demanding a constant supply of junk food. It's no wonder we fight a losing battle against them.

Sleep. Sleep is our body's inbuilt repair system. While we're asleep, our negative thoughts, painful emotions and compulsive behaviour, stops. This allows balance to be restored.

Unfortunately, we do our best to sabotage this system. We mess up our body's ability to sleep by staring at the artificial light on our phones, and by consuming stim-

FEED ME!

BREAKING BAD BACTERIA

ulants like caffeine, alcohol and sugar. These ensure we don't get the kind of deep sleep our body needs to do its job.

Movement. We are designed to move, not sit around most of the time at desks, in coffee shops, or on the couch. Exercise is one of the quickest ways to lift depression. It stimulates blood flow and gets oxygen into the body, which makes us feel more alive. It connects the left and right hemispheres of the brain, which helps balance and clarity of thought.

All movement is good... Yoga. Martial arts. Walking. Dancing. Running. Playing. Our mind brain will reason that we are tired, so we should conserve what little energy we have. Our gut brain knows that our body can generate energy, particularly when it's moving – unfortunately it's been lulled to sleep with Netflix and pizza.

Breathing. We transact with the world around us through our breath. We breathe in oxygen and breathe out carbon dioxide. Trees breathe in carbon dioxide and breathe out oxygen. Breathing is essential to life, yet we barely pay attention to it. Most of our breathing is unconscious and far too shallow. When we're stressed, anxious or depressed, we barely breathe at all.

Our cells need the oxygen of deep breaths, to give us energy and to eliminate toxins. Conscious breathing has the power to completely change our state of mind. If we want more energy we can make the in-breath longer than the out-breath. If we want to be more relaxed, we can make the out-breath longer than the in-breath.

Also, it's a good idea to breathe outside. It's beneficial to spend time connecting to living things rather than pixelated ones; more time in sunlight than blue light. Walking in nature is perfect for this. It gives us hope that there is life, and it seems to be intelligent.

Meditation. The biggest stumbling block to developing a relationship with the life force through the gut brain is the constant, distracting chatter of the mind. It convinces us that there are far more important things to be doing than moving our body, breathing consciously, sleeping when tired or eating food that has recently been alive. A meditation practice increases awareness of the body by quieting the mind, with its impulsive, child like demands to be heard.

For years I researched the latest, cutting edge techniques for increasing energy... super-foods, super supplements (SO expensive), super mitochondria healing processes. I must have read over a million words on the subject... while eating cake and drinking lattes. My mind wanted "super, special, dramatic" not ordinary, but when you sum up all the books and webinars, unfortunately it comes down to these simple things, done with consistency.

Manage creative energy – the dark force stuff

Facing our fear of consequence

We control our creative expression, because spontaneity is a risky business... particularly if we want to avoid humiliation, and we REALLY want to avoid humiliation. We block our connection to the life force, in case it delivers messages we don't want to hear.

We override our intuitive hits until eventually we don't hear them any more. We say we like surprises, but really we just want to be surprised by things we know and like, which isn't really in keeping with the "surprise" element.

We say we like honesty, but we don't like being unpopular, so we avoid speaking the truth. This means our words say one thing, but our energy, when denied expression, becomes passive aggressive. Most people these days prefer true expression to passive aggression. "Right now I feel like I want to kill you" is unlikely to be taken literally. It's also preferable to swallowing the hand grenade yourself, and wondering when the pin will work its way loose.

The reason we don't express ourselves creatively or spontaneously is because we don't want to fail and look stupid.

Become more aware

We hide all our dark secrets in the gut... our lies, our guilt for hurting others, and our desire for revenge when others hurt or humiliate us. We hide our feelings about sex and money – insecurity about our desirability, fear of not having enough money, envy that others have more. Shame, guilt and revenge pull us down into the low frequency energies of rage and depression (which is a form of rage against ourselves).

But if we stay on the surface, all our "goodness" is fake. It's shallow goodness. We have to meet our rage before we can truly rise above it. This is a bit like the philosophy of martial arts. Work towards becoming a black belt killing machine, in order to become the most peaceful man in the room. Another paradox.

KILLER PRESENCE

Many of the fears in our gut come from old patterns. In our ancient history, we spent a lot of time under threat from wild animals and marauding tribes. Death was never far away.

Currently we fear "dying on stage" aka humiliation. This is a problem because "all the world's a stage" which means the grim reaper is around every corner.

We're paralyzed by indecision because though our upgraded mind brain can make individual choices, it can't process all the consequences of these choices. The intuitive intelligence in our body is far better suited to the task, but we're disconnected from it.

This is like swapping the old lamp containing the genie of unlimited creativity, for a new one, which, though it has a brightly impressive identity, is empty and devoid of all magic.

If we start to transform our bad habits – physical bad habits (eating, sleeping, moving, breathing) and mental bad habits (negative thinking, fearful thinking) our energetic set point changes. We're no longer running a program of self destruction. This sends a message to our inner Sorcerer that it can wake up now. We're a safe pair of hands. We'll use our increased power for creativity, not destruction. We'll be a trustworthy vessel for the life force.

Most people who have achieved this, describe the encounter as bliss.

If you seek wisdom,
Be silent

If you seek peace,
Be still

If you seek love,
Be yourself

CHAPTER 25

The Mantras

Sometimes we don't have half an hour to do yoga, or meditate, or walk in nature, even though it's been said that if you're really busy, that's when you need to do the whole hour. I know this advice doesn't make sense in our dimension, but I do know that it works.

Luckily, there is a fast way to get into alignment... mantras! A mantra is a focused thought, which can quickly change our energy and raise our vibration. Mantras are quick tools we can use whenever we start to spiral downwards.

To keep things simple, I've included one for each energy centre.

The mind – *"Thank you"*

The heart – *"I love you"*

The gut – *"I'm sorry"*

The words *Thank you, I love you* and *I'm sorry* have been devalued in recent times.

We're raised to say *thank you*, as a form of politeness... as a means to get people to like us or approve of us. The deeper thank you is more difficult to do because it's less self-serving. It's a thank you to life, the whole of life (which means being thankful for things we don't want). This kind of *thank you* stretches our mind.

With practice this comes easier. As Sam Harris says "Right now, there are at least a billion people who'd consider all their prayers answered if they could trade places with you." Sometimes we forget to appreciate what we've already got.

There is now scientific evidence that the practice of gratitude actually rewires the neurons in the brain. Because our cells are being replaced all the time, we actually have the means to become higher vibrational beings. The upgrade costs nothing, and is just a thought away... a Thank You away.

If someone else gets the job we want, saying an internal *thank you* seems crazy, but that's because we can only see what's happening here and now. We can't see what's coming. We could trust that a much better plan is unfolding.

Unfortunately, without this trust, we usually respond with emotions of anger or disappointment. This changes our energetic set point and sends us off course, which means we miss what's being lined up. Then we get to say "Life sucks" rather than what's more truthful "I keep messing with the Sat Nav".

The words *I love you* have been devalued in a similar way. Lovers say "I love you" and require an *I love you* back, in fact they can become sulky when it isn't forthcoming. It's a needy *I love you*. Friends say *I love you* as a substitute for "goodbye" or "see you later". The deeper *I love you* is more difficult and less self-serving. It's the kind that loves unconditionally – even though the object of our love doesn't return that love. This kind of *I love you* stretches our heart.

If someone hurts or disappoints us, it seems crazy to say *I love you* because the inner feeling is more like "I hate you, how could you do this to me". These aren't necessarily feelings, they're emotions. Emotions are always lined up on the side of identity, not energy. They're like spinning tops. Just when you think they're slowing down, a quick swipe (a single thought) can get them spinning all over again.

Love will always trigger neediness, because this was our original state when we first experienced love. Probably our earliest sense memory of duality is "I am love – this feels amazing", followed quickly by "I am separate from love – this feels terrifying". Real love comes with no fear attached. It can't leave because it's who we are. The opportunity for us to experience this has been brought to us in the guise of another person (regardless of what they choose to do next).

We say *I'm sorry* to change the atmosphere from hostile to pleasant. The deeper *I'm sorry* is more difficult because it requires us to really own the very difficult feelings of guilt (for the pain we caused), and humiliation (for the shame of being found out).

If someone hurts us it's painful, but it's even more painful to know that we are the cause of another's suffering. That's why we disconnect and go into denial. When we make mistakes in life (inevitable because we're only human) people get hurt. We lie, to minimize our part in the hurt, or apologise as quickly as possible, so we don't have to feel the guilt and humiliation in our gut.

This disowned energy wrecks our immune system and prevents us from really experiencing life. Guilt and humiliation are hideous, but avoidance makes them stronger. Save yourself the time. ... say *"I'm sorry"*. Then burn, and cry and burn through it some more. Eventually it does go away.

* * *

When the planes were about to fly into the twin towers, everyone knew they were going to die, and so they made their last phone calls. It's illuminating to hear what was expressed. In all instances it was some variation of *I love you... Thank you... I'm sorry*. Nobody wanted to win, get revenge or check how many "likes" their last post got. There was a similar outpouring of love on the ground. People who normally rushed around New York, eyes fixed on their target or disconnected by whatever was streaming into their headphones, were hugging, helping each other, sharing resources.

I love you... Thank you... I'm sorry. Let's not wait for a disaster, when we could spend as much time as possible saying these things now.

CHAPTER 26

The virtual Monolith

No-one knows for sure what caused the last leap forward in evolution. A black monolith; Eve eating an apple from the tree of knowledge; or a superior race arriving from another planet who genetically modified the Neanderthals.

The latter is not so crazy. It could explain our split personality of being part animal/part higher conscious being. Our dubious ancient parentage could also be the origin of the "Virgin Birth" idea, a feature of many different religions and mythologies, in which superior beings are born without going through any normal conception process.

Now that (even with our limited intelligence) we've cloned sheep and created labra-doodles this isn't all that far fetched. Also given that there are over 100 billion stars in our galaxy and there are trillions of galaxies, the fact that there is a more advanced species than us is kind of inevitable. When we look around our planet, I doubt we are the pinnacle of God's creation.

Regardless of how it happened, we know that the last leap forward in evolution was marked by three things.

1 An opposable thumb

With an opposable thumb, our early ancestors were able to hold things. In 2001 A Space Odyssey this meant holding a femur bone with which to bludgeon another tribe member. Over time, this capability extended to wielding swords for combat or using knives for cutting steak. Eventually we got to holding pens and paintbrushes and we saved lives doing precision surgery with scalpels.

2 Communication

Communication between primates was limited to grunts and shrieks. With the arrival of our neocortex we developed words, and then whole sentences. Eventually we were able to express ourselves through literature and poetry.

3 Fire

Rubbing two sticks together (facilitated by the opposable thumb) led to the invention of fire. This meant that early man could now barbecue meat and read (his newly discovered words) after the sun went down. Eventually this led to the invention of the steam engine and the industrial revolution. After that we were off to the races.

Our next leap forward in evolution could involve a similar trio, but updated for the 21st Century...

1 An opposable mind

Roger Martin of Toronto University coined this phrase. It relates to a Scott Fitzgerald quote "The test of a first rate intelligence is the ability to hold two opposing ideas in mind at the same time, and still retain the ability to function."

We have two hemispheres of the brain (left and right) and each functions in a slightly different way. Previously the world favoured the attributes of the left side – the micro... attention to detail, focus, logic. This is often referred to as the Masculine side.

More recently, the emphasis has been on the right side – the macro... creativity, empathy, the relationship between ideas, rather than the ideas themselves. This is often referred to as the Feminine side. Many skills of the left brain are now done better by computers. Once a computer was able to beat the best chess player in the world, it seemed a bit pointless to spend too much time learning to process data.

However rather than fighting over which side is better, scientists have now found that the superior brain is one with the most *connections* between left and right. We need to practice integration if we want an expanded brain. We do this by breaking habitual thinking patterns and getting comfortable with contrasting ideas. If we hold two opposing ideas in balance, without rushing to a conclusion, something completely new can drop into the gap between them. This thought comes from the metaphysical realm, rather than our inner data bank. It's often described as "Genius".

Scientists have also found that when we think unfamiliar thoughts i.e. we stop fearful, repetitive thoughts and replace them with positive or imaginative thoughts, we turn on new genes. As we're creating ourselves all the time, this is a very good thing.

This "opposable mind" could lead to as many new discoveries and talents, as our previous "opposable thumbs" did... in a fraction of the time, due to our increasingly sophisticated technology.

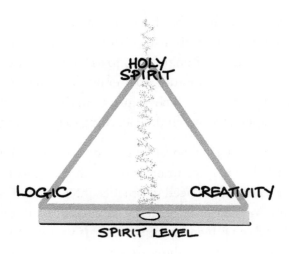

2 A different form of communication

Now that the terms emotional intelligence and passive aggression have entered our vocabulary, we are more aware of the energy behind words, rather than the words themselves.

Language can be used to manipulate and confuse. The 2008 financial crash opened everyone's eyes to what was really going on... to the fact that money didn't actually exist, it was just an idea, a balloon that popped, an opioid dream we woke up from. The opium sellers faced no consequences. Confidence (in both corporations and government) was shattered beyond redemption. And yet we carried on... business as usual. Except deep down we're still really, really angry.

We already have phrases like "the letter of the law" versus "the spirit of the law" but after any corporate corruption is exposed, people shrug and say "We knew it was wrong, but all the letters were in the right order, the boxes were ticked, so what could we do?"

After the Jimmy Savile paedophilia scandal broke, hundreds of people came forward and said "We knew he was evil, it was OBVIOUS, but what could we do? Letters after his name. Plaques on the wall". These people were reading the energy, not the identity.

We need to learn the language of energy, so that we can sense intention or the energy *behind* the words.

As we enter the metaphysical realm, and we develop our capacity to read energy, the communication of the future will be more intuitive. Intuitive perception would bring a whole new meaning to the idea of transparency. We will probably look back on this time and realize what a blunt instrument words were.

3 The fire of creativity

It takes practice and commitment to update our software program from survival to creativity. For thousands of years our consciousness was more animal than divine, more survival than creative. We had to err on the side of caution and fear in order to stay alive.

If we heard a "bustle in the hedgerow" our body would flood with adrenaline, ready to fight or run away. If, on the other hand, we said "That's given me an idea for a song about the May Queen" we might be dead a few minutes later. There's no point penning *Stairway to Heaven* if you're about to be eaten by a lion. (Still such a Led Zeppelin fan).

This danger/stress response is fine for animals, because after the threat has gone away, the adrenaline dissipates and they go back to eating grass. It's not fine for humans because we have a creative neocortex, which is able to IMAGINE stressful scenarios, even when there's no physical threat. We're anxious all the time.

When we're flooded with the chemicals of stress, our creative brain switches off and our survival brain takes over. The energy we would normally use to attack or run away gets turned in on ourselves. We become self destructive, or we leave our body energetically, so that we're no longer present.

The logical part of our mind finds the tension of stress unbearable, but the creative part loves tension. It's the grit that makes the pearl in the oyster. If we stay present while taking deep breaths to calm the fear in our gut, a new idea can drop in. If a stone is dropped into turbulent water, it has no effect, but if a stone is dropped into still water, it's ripples extend far and wide. Genius ideas are available to us, but our energy needs to be still enough to receive them.

With an open mind, we can receive intuition. With an open heart we can fuel our creative ideas with passion and enthusiasm. Enthusiasm comes from the Greek "En theos" meaning "In God"... sometimes words ARE cool.

* * *

The world is now changing at exponential speed and we're still clinging to out of date ways of doing just about everything.

According to data analysis, falsehoods spread six times faster than truth on the internet. Fear and technology are a dangerous combination. Technology moves too fast to be regulated by legislation. By the time the legislation has been drafted, it's out of date. Also, governments don't even understand the technology, so how could they regulate what they don't understand.

On a metaphysical level, we have the most sophisticated computer in the world inside our body, and we use it to text and play video games. 95% of this computer (our consciousness) is unknown to us. It's there, but we just haven't tapped into it yet. It's important to remember this when we feel powerless against The Man.

At the moment our inner slave is becoming even more enslaved. Mikhail Aleksandrovich Bakunin summarized this "In antiquity, slaves were called slaves. In the middle ages, they took the name serfs. Nowadays they are called users".

The Man no longer wants our physical labour but our attention, our "eyeballs", our data. With this data, he can hijack our power of choice by tapping into our specific needs and fears. We think we have free will to make independent choices, but we're being subtly programmed.

Unscrupulous corporations use technology to separate us, prey on our fears and steal elections. They fragment society with rumours, gossip and targeted ads. We live in echo chambers. We think we're listening to objective world news but actually it's more like a Spotify playlist on repeat.

If we wake up from the trance, we could use technology to join together in more creative ways. Gone are the days of "Rich man in the castle, pauper at the gate". A pauper with a smart phone can change the world. We can rise above duality if we meet and integrate the energy. All the energy...

Mind, Heart and Gut.
Masculine and Feminine.
Animal nature and Divine nature.

If these came together, we'd be a force to be reckoned with...

Result – species upgrade.

CHAPTER 27

Hey, hey we're the Monkeys

I can't remember where I first heard the term "Not my monkeys, not my circus" but it kind of sums up the philosophy you need to get things done these days. Monkeys are problems, and you shouldn't get involved with them if they're not your responsibility.

Sometimes we get drawn in, because monkeys are very distracting, and cute, in a chaotic sort of way. They create a lot of drama, which is very compelling. Unfortunately, this phrase can also give us the idea that we should stay clear of **all** monkeys, and in fact we should avoid the circus altogether.

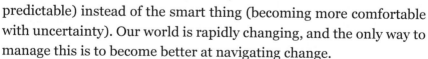

We know life is uncertain and unpredictable, yet we keep doing the stupid thing (we try to make it predictable) instead of the smart thing (becoming more comfortable with uncertainty). Our world is rapidly changing, and the only way to manage this is to become better at navigating change.

It's like the "teach a man to fish" analogy, only this time, you teach him to manage energy... that way you won't be dealing with a lifetime of damage limitation.

Scientists have always known that our brains are smaller than our ape like ancestors, but a recent discovery has shown that the genetic difference between us and Neanderthals, is the same as the one that separates dogs from wolves and cattle from bison. In other words, once the wolves and bison were domesticated, something happened genetically and their brains became smaller.

We know that humans domesticated dogs and cattle, but who domesticated us 100,000 years ago?! This could add to the debate about whether we were in fact visited by an advanced species. If this is the case, it could account for our tendency to become enslaved by the spells of The Man. Perhaps in the future, we'll look back on ourselves and wonder why we put up with The Man for so long, then we'll watch a Labrador shake hands and play dead in exchange for a dog biscuit, and it'll all make sense.

The other monkey phrase that became very popular a while ago was the one that featured A Hundred Monkeys. This is the strange phenomenon that if you teach one monkey to wash a banana, other monkeys copy him. When you get to 100 monkeys, monkeys in other countries (monkeys who've never seen each other) start washing their bananas.

This bodes well for humanity, just in case we were feeling slightly overwhelmed about the way we're not getting the evolution thing. All it takes is 100 really conscious people to connect with each other, and the ripples of a new way of doing life could spread across the globe.

Right now, people are craving connection more than ever... deep, intimate connection. Loneliness has become a big problem – as has anti social behavior. We could blame the internet or The Man for this, because between them they offer up all kinds of *counterfeit connection* like technology, food and alcohol. The Man employs an army of experts to create "crave-ability" (yes it's their word). They have the science (though not the morals) to do this.

Technology, food and alcohol offer fake connection to a best friend who is...

Always there when there's something to celebrate.
120 Likes you smashed it!
Let's eat cake.
Who's for cocktails?

Always there when there's something to rage against.
Share this post!
Where's the nachos?
Open the wine.

Always there when we're alone and sad.
Everyone's doing so much better than me. This is a bad day. I may as well ruin it completely with Netflix, binge eating and tequila.

Technology reinforces our identity by feeding back to us everything we've ever said "yes" to. In effect it says "this is who you are... someone who likes these films, these websites, has these opinions, buys these products, comments on these threads, is friends with these people". This can create an illusion of security "I know who I am when I'm connected to my smart phone".

It also means we become uncomfortable interacting with the real world. Other people make us feel energy we don't like – irritation, anger, boredom. But pushing through these feelings allows something new to emerge – a kind of joy in the actual feeling of being alive.

We can feel isolated and lonely in a room full of people, and we can feel existentially lonely in a room full of technology. One isn't better than the other, but the technology will keep us in safe mode, whereas the people will make us react. Where there's reaction, there's energy. And where there's energy, there's the possibility for transformation.

We're human beings, and we need to bond with other human beings. They may be chaotic and unpredictable, but if we develop a sense of humour, learn some juggling skills and become a better ringmaster, we could find out that this is our circus after all.

CHAPTER 28

Rage. Adoration and the invention of Cool

The story of the Summer of Love wouldn't be complete without a mention of The Beatles. Obviously their music was brilliant, but they were extraordinary for another reason... Beatlemania.

The music that came before The Beatles moved people... jazz prompted them to dance; brass bands made them proud; folk music encouraged laughter; classical music elevated them to wistful reverence. But the Beatles produced... hysteria.

It's hard to explain Beatlemania from the standpoint of the identity world. Of course they had an identity (funny hair cuts and collarless suits) but nobody understood the screaming that greeted them everywhere they went, because this was coming from the energy world.

Their girl fans would stare wide-eyed in the throws of an ecstasy they didn't understand. They would swoon and cry... but mostly they would scream. The Beatles were a catalyst, waking up an energy in them that was so strong they couldn't hold it in their body and had to release it in a primal way. It's a perfect example of the intensity of awakening feminine energy – the adoration, that's on the other side of rage.

Security didn't know what to do with it. The industry didn't know what to do with it. Parents didn't know what to do with it. And then the phenomenon went away. There are a few possible reasons for this, one of which may be fear.

As we have seen in a previous chapter, female hysteria has been associated with the negative identities of mad people and witches. In other words people who can't be controlled. As they grew up, girls didn't want to be associated with that.

The enterprising world picked up on this and matched Beatlemania with its counterpart... the invention of Cool. Cool is the opposite of hysterical, it's sexy. Cool has also allowed the Man to become very wealthy.

In the Disney film *Fantasia*, Mickey Mouse is a sorcerer's apprentice. Tasked with mopping the floor when his Master leaves the house, he opens a book of spells hoping to use magic to do the job for him. The result is disaster as hundreds of mops and pails of water go completely out of control.

Watching videos of Beatlemania is somewhat similar. The Beatles opened the spell book and unleashed a coven of untrained sorcerers. It's no wonder we were so quick to put Pandora back in her box.

In the same way that Religion kept young people in line by inculcating them with guilt, the identity world keeps young people in line by inculcating them with "cool". They're both spells that eclipse the power of reasoning.

The need to be cool, suppresses energy, and nowhere is this more evident than in social media. Photographs that express energy don't make it to social media if the facial expressions are unflattering. The energy may shriek "we're having an amazing time" but if we want the picture to make us look cool, we settle for posed pictures of fake joy.

It's interesting to watch our identity doing its thing. First we place a "cool" overlay on top of our true essence, then we place a "zany" layer on top of the cool layer. We work at getting the mix just right... exuberant, but not ridiculous; doe eyes and jazz hands. It's a tricky balancing act.

It's no wonder we fall in love with musicians on stage (off stage they're not so compelling). When they play they are completely absorbed in something else. They're connected to their muse/the divine/the source of creativity. With less "self" in the way, life force energy can flow through them. We long for that state, because it's the opposite of what we are experiencing (self consciousness).

Musicians who keep a band together (the Beatles for a while, Bruce Springsteen for an era) have the added benefit of "when two or more are gathered, there I am". Not only do they lose their sense of personal identity, they also lose the anxiety of choice. They play together instinctively, knowing what each will do a split second beforehand. They become one unified being, containing separate individuals... in other words a Holy Trinity, that allows genius level flow.

It's easy to be a solo player in life (regardless of what kind of work we do) because the company of other humans will always trigger the rage of our inner demons. Of course, once they're tamed, they bring with them a lot of powerful energy (hence the phenomenon of Bruce Springsteen's live show).

We're wired for connection. Connecting to the external world often makes us miserable. (*Am I ok? Do you like me? Do you think I'm smart, interesting, sexy?*) Connecting to the source of creativity, on the other hand, makes us feel fully alive.

We all have life force energy inside us, but we keep it under lock and key in case we make mistakes with it. We're scared of being spontaneous, scared of being judged and found to be uncool... so we engage with the world from behind the safety glass of a smart phone.

Fear of judgment comes from an affinity with the Old Testament God, who loved dividing people into good or bad, because he only had two places to put them – Heaven or Hell. A place for winners, and a place for losers.

The energy world operates by different rules. A simple story describes this best... A western man travelled to Africa. He was charmed by the way young African boys would run and play so athletically. He offered a prize of a bag of sweets to the fastest runner in the group. They were to race to a tree 200 metres away. At the sound of the starting gun, the boys held hands and ran to the finish line together. The man thought them simple, because they didn't understand the rules of the game. But while sharing out the sweets, they asked how one of them could be happy if the others lost. The prize wouldn't be worth having. The sweets could not be enjoyed.

We have forgotten this simple truth. In our desire to prove ourselves as winners, we have forgotten how to play... how to let life "play" us. We have forgotten the bliss of being possessed by the life force. We swap this freedom of spirit for control, and a "cool" identity.

It's a very bad trade.

Each of us is unique, but we swap unique for "special". Special is part of the identity world, it means better than others. The drive for special-ness separates us, whereas the fact that we're all unique unites us. Our individual charisma is in a category of "one" so it defies measurement. It can therefore connect to others without jostling for power. It can create a whole that's greater than the sum of the parts.

Charisma comes from the Greek word meaning "grace or talent from God". Though it's part of the metaphysical realm, we try to reach it through the physical one. We see it in other people, and we yearn for them, but what we're really yearning for is our own charisma... we want to be in a relationship with our own soul, and the grace that comes with that.

Imagine what our life would feel like if we lost our self consciousness and experienced ourselves in a flow of energy that is powerful, playful, loving, creative and inclusive.

The future is feminine. Not ineffective, sweet or manipulative femi-nine. Not limited to gender, or driven by an agenda. Not frightened of rage or adoration... the kind of feminine that could give birth to a whole new world.

CHAPTER 29

How life works

As energy beings, we are all co-creators, but as physical beings we want to control this process as much as possible.

If we spontaneously express ourselves, we hate the uncertain feeling this gives us, so we try to get to the next moment as quickly as possible. As Dorothy Parker once said "I hate writing, I love having written". On the other hand, if we deny our creative spirit, and default to habit mode, we feel a sense of loss.

Deep inside we have an inner force that seeks outer expression. Our identity tries to condense this expression into some form of physical representation (e.g. words on paper, paint on canvas, title on business card) so that it can be judged and valued. But our creative spirit doesn't need validation, it just wants a way to play in this three dimensional world for the sheer joy of experience.

We perceive life the wrong way around. We think life happens to us... events happen, and we respond to them. For example, if we fail a job interview, and we're disappointed or angry, we think the unsuccessful interview caused these bad feelings.

In reality it works like this...

The job interview goes badly. We have thoughts... *I fucked it up. She was horrible. Why did I say that. I have no talent. Life is so unfair. There's no point trying. How will I make rent next month.* These thoughts make us feel angry, sad or humiliated. These emotions cause our gut to release stress hormones. These hormones cause our mind to think fearful, angry or depressed thoughts, so the cycle continues until it becomes automatic.

Our unhappiness comes from our thinking about the events, not from the events themselves. Because we disconnected from our creative spirit, most of the time we're not having a direct experience of life, we're just having an experience of our thoughts, and the emotions those thoughts create.

Repeated thoughts become embedded as an attitude. Now our entire energy system is vibrating at the low frequency vibrations of apathy, cynicism, anger or fear... even without our conscious awareness. Because we're electromagnetic beings, we attract things of a similar frequency, which means we're cut off from inspiration, love and creativity. We then have to use willpower to get anything done, which is exhausting.

An alternative scenario could go like this...

We fail a job interview, and PAUSE, feeling the direct hit of the disappointment in our gut and our heart. Without thoughts adding fuel to the fire, the energy of anger, sadness or fear burns itself out and leaves our body. Into this void we could introduce creative or loving thoughts or even just "Ok, now what's next?" thoughts. This would lead to a very different outcome.

Having no thoughts is an acquired skill so it's helpful to start with noticing our thoughts; noticing the way we're always trying to get to the next moment; noticing the way we sabotage good feelings. Happiness is fleeting. Love brings the possibility of loss. We don't like this uncertainty, so we let go of the good feelings because it's much easier to control bad feelings than good ones.

It seems crazy to say we're more familiar with negative thoughts and feelings than positive ones but a couple of simple exercises make this clear...

1   Take two pieces of paper. On one piece write down all the negative thoughts that go through your mind. Imagine all the things you say to yourself, when you're bored, when people are unkind, when things go wrong, when you make mistakes, when you wish you'd done something differently, when you're lazy, when you eat junk food.

   Take the second piece of paper and write down all the positive thoughts that go through your mind. Imagine all the things you say to yourself when you're proud of yourself, when people are kind, when you do things well, when you're praised by colleagues or complimented by friends, when you make an effort.

Now look at the ratio of positive words to negative words and see how unkind the mind is when left to its own devices.

2   Remember an event that caused you to feel a negative feeling – a heartbreak, a betrayal or a humiliation. Start the clock and see how long you can hold onto the feeling. You can insert thoughts to add fuel to the fire. Notice how easy it is to keep this going.

   Next, remember an event that caused you to feel a positive feeling – happiness, bliss, excitement. See how long you can hold onto this feeling. You know already that it's a fraction of the time of the former, but doing the exercise really brings the message home.

We need to get creative, happy, loving thoughts into our gut so they take root and become more automatic.

Thinking uses a lot of energy. In order to conserve energy, we have an "automatic pilot". If we see something for the first time, we're curious,

211

so we think a lot *What is it? What does it do? Where did it come from? Who made it? Etc.* When we see it for the second time, our data bank flashes up an image that represents all the information we have previously gathered so we don't have to think. It's an efficient system.

The "automatic pilot" also drives our behaviour. In order to choose which things to turn over to the automatic pilot, our gut brain presumes it's whatever we do most frequently, like breathing or brushing our teeth. This is good news for our teeth, but terrible news for our unhealthy habits, whether that's eating junk food, scrolling through social media, or just worrying about the future.

The reason we need to *practice* creative thinking and *practice* loving feelings, is to get the gut brain to notice how frequently we're doing them. Once this happens, it sends them to the "automatic pilot". Then life gets easier. Freedom becomes possible.

When we break a habit, we start to develop self esteem. This leads to happier emotions. Happier emotions lead to more creative, inspired thoughts. High vibration thoughts gives us access to our Holy Spirit. This ends the anxiety of choice, because our decisions are now guided by a superior intelligence.

Once this happens, we no longer need to escape ourselves because being present is so much more interesting.

Real freedom is freedom from negative thoughts, painful emotions and compulsive behaviours. It's a goal worth reaching for. If God is the force of love, that created us, and gave us evolutionary potential to overcome our lower survival nature and rise to our divine one... then this gender neutral force will probably laugh and say "go you... absolutely smashed it!" or perhaps "this is my beloved, in whom I am well pleased".

Words are transitory, subjective, unimportant things. The only thing that's real... is love.

CHAPTER 30

David Bowie –
the day the music died

This story started with David Bowie so it's fitting to finish with him. In his too short life, The Man Who Fell to Earth, seemed to live many lifetimes.

He epitomized the new metaphysical paradigm that this book describes, and the new kind of hero we need to become – a combination of hero and heroine.

He became the child Jesus referred to in "unless you become as little children you cannot enter the kingdom of heaven". When responding to the "Who are you?" question that hounds so many of us, he said "Who I am is my enthusiasms".

His enthusiasms were many and varied because he was interested in creativity, not money, status or success. Ironically of course, they came as a by product, because that's how metaphysics works. The life force responds to our energy, not our C.V, our bank balance or our earnest requests for more.

While retaining the curiosity of the child, he became addicted to cocaine and alcohol, but this didn't stop him. He went to the edges and depths and came back, conquering both addictions only to become stronger. He met, rescued and integrated his inner damsel.

While retaining the imagination of the child, he was massively stolen from and betrayed by The Man, but he didn't fall into a pit of despair or rage. He just kept going... kept creating. He faced the dark side of sorcery and held onto his light.

While retaining the creativity of the child, he played a multitude of characters to inspire, enrich and entertain us. He became a master of transformation, because he had no need to capitalize on any one of these identities. He wasn't interested in "building a brand" or becoming trapped in one identity. He kept moving, kept evolving, kept asking "what next?"

He balanced his masculine and feminine sides. Not in his androgynous identity, but in his energy... his approach to life.

He could finesse the details in the micro, and take in the broader picture of the macro. He was single minded and focused when working on his art, while staying open to being informed and inspired by the world. He was driven to individual excellence, but he also championed the creativity of others.

Being a Knight of the energy realm, Bowie turned down a knighthood from the Queen – the old world of identity just wasn't relevant to him.

He lived in the "now" moment, creating for the joy of it, refusing to be limited, contained or pigeonholed. Throughout his life he drew from everywhere – literature, art, fashion, philosophy and ultimately mysticism and love.

He didn't copy stuff that was cool. He got in touch with the essence of what made him who he was. After that, anything he embraced became cool by association... androgeny, knitted jumpsuits, facepaint. He even made Germany sexy.

Essence isn't an identity, it's a vibration, an energetic thumb print that can't be copied or condensed.

Curious mind. Courageous heart. Creative depth.

Bowie was a hero for our times. Unlike Johnny Rotten, he didn't lose faith and descend to a world marked by cynicism, endless opinions, and the marketing of butter.

Perhaps he recognized that he was a slave, as we all are, somewhere in our DNA. However he made the ultimate journey – becoming a slave to the rhythm of life. Instead of being a victim, he surrendered into something bigger, and got carried along for the ride. He got to direct the energy, which was ultimately his greatest achievement.

He was a true sorcerer.

And now it's our turn to pick up the gauntlet.

Everything in the world is inside out. It seems as if we're experiencing the world, but we're only ever experiencing our own energy. Something happens and we feel joy; something else happens and we feel pain, but these feelings were inside us all along... the world just hit a particular chord and we felt the vibration of that. The world is "playing" us, like a musical instrument.

In order to create an interesting life, we need to be open to an experience of all the notes. Power chords are energizing, minor keys are poignant, melodies are joyful. If we try to control life, we limit the extent to which life can "play" us. If we're limited to a repertoire of three chords, our music could be banal or boring. Life would be more *Frog Chorus* and less *Diamond Dogs*.

Living in the technological age, we are surrounded by stimuli. We're subjected to more conversations, more words, more images in an hour than previous generations processed in a year, so our natural response is to be defensive, not open. We "surf" the net, we "scan" emails, we "glance" at Instagram. We don't let anything go deep. This means a cacophony of surface noise, yet we feel no vibration. We're disconnected from the field of intelligence that lies just beyond our five senses.

If we live in the energy world and allow life to play us, we experience all the notes. After that we can pick up the baton and start conducting. It's no accident that a conductor directs an orchestra and a conductor is a channel for energy; no accident that the baton looks like a magic wand, transforming hundreds of different notes and chords in different keys, into a symphony... the full expression of who we really are.

We could be heroes.

We could create something new, different and beautiful.

If we rise, mighty forces will come to our aid.

David Bowie died on 10th January 2016. He kept on creating until the time of his departure. He was, and is Lazarus. I can only presume he was wanted in another galaxy, because he certainly blazed a trail in this one.

Who we are is not of this world. Who we are is the one experiencing this world.

Let's make it a memorable experience.

Lightning Source UK Ltd.
Milton Keynes UK
UKHW022208281019
352468UK00008B/262/P